Dear Family,
    May the G
the gift of hea
Voice.
            Blessings,
            Sanjay Prajapati

M000017250

EARTH, WIND, FIRE, & A STILL SMALL VOICE

HOW TO HEAR THE VOICE OF GOD

SANJAY PRAJAPATI
2-Time #1 Best Selling Author

Copyright © 2018 by Sanjay Prajapati

Discover the blueprint to destiny at:

www.Destined4Torah.com

[Deuteronomy 4:32-33 NKJV] "32 "For ask now concerning the days that are past, which were before you, since the day that God created man on the earth, and [ask] from one end of heaven to the other, whether [any] great [thing] like this has happened, or [anything] like it has been heard. 33 "Did [any] people [ever] hear the voice of God speaking out of the midst of the fire, as you have heard, and live?"

TABLE OF CONTENTS

FOREWORD BY DR. MICHELLE CORRAL

Have you ever wondered how to hear God's voice? Have you ever asked the question, am I hearing God's voice correctly?

The incredible revelation and Torah truth of God's Word in this book will help you receive that answer. This book is established to help you to know God's voice and to walk in the path of truth that you have desired. It will abet you to becoming more prophetic and enable you to walk in the paths of righteousness. You will learn about Elijah and so many other Prophets that listened to the Word of God including the Talmudim that were trained by them.

Pastor Sanjay also known as Rabbi Sanjay is one of the most articulate Torah teachers that I know. His book, "Earth, Wind, Fire, & A Still Small Voice" is one of the most incredible Torah tools that you can receive on hearing the voice of God.

The method that Pastor Sanjay uses is closely associated with the early Prophets in the way that they traditionally taught Torah. His method of teaching can also be compared to a Master Torah Scholar that will teach us how to hear God's voice in a most incredible manner.

I highly recommend every believer to thoroughly read this book and make it part of your spiritual itinerary and armament. It will take you to the highest-level Torah study, not just in the basic pshat (simple-understanding) level, but it will bring you to a place of Sod (Secret), as it written in a God's word,

[AMOS 3:7 KJV] "7 SURELY THE LORD GOD WILL DO NOTHING, BUT HE REVEALETH HIS SECRET UNTO HIS SERVANTS THE PROPHETS."

Pastor Sanjay is one of those servants and Prophets who has been gifted by God to receive the utmost revelation of God's Word. His prophetic insight and years of Torah study has allowed him to write this extraordinary book that I believe will change the lives of every believer.

Dr. Michelle Corral

ACKNOWLEDGMENTS

I am grateful for Dr. Michelle Corral. She has been my Pastor, Torah teacher, and mentor since 1991. There are no words to express my gratitude. This book would not have been possible without all of her support. This book is the fruit of her labor. I thank the Lord for her continual support. Dr. Corral is the foundress of Breath of the Spirit Ministries International and Breath of the Spirit Prophetic Word Center, located in Yorba Linda, California. She is also the foundress of Chesed International, the Humanitarian Branch of Breath of the Spirit. Chesed provides daily feeding programs to children in the Philippines, Kenya, and Haiti. It also offers daily feeding to the elderly in Zambia. Chesed also provides water wells in Africa and ongoing medical missions in the Philippines, Kenya, Zambia, Haiti, Sierra Leone, Egypt, Burundi and Uganda. Dr. Corral is also the foundress of the Father's Treasure Orphan home in Haiti. In addition to Dr. Corral's weekly telecast The Prophetic Word, which currently airs on The Word Network, she continues to have a strong television presence. I encourage you to financially support her work around the world at: http://drmichellecorral.net/our_work.html.

I am grateful for Reverend Donyale Dabney for all her support. I really appreciate all of her talents in editing and revising the book. She has spent countless hours in editing and revising both of my books. Rev. Donyale is the founder of Testimony Times International Ministries. Testimony Times International Ministries has humbly and graciously accepted the call to be used as a vehicle to display the wonderful and mighty works of God. Through Testimony Times Newspaper, Testimony Times TV/Radio, Testimony Times Conferences, and Testimony Times Missions. God has commissioned her to go out into the world to declare that He is still a miracle working God who is moving by His power every day. I invite you to visit her facebook page at: https://www.facebook.com/pg/Testimony-Times-International-Ministries-211620005596232/

I am grateful for the constant love and support of my beautiful wife, Bhavna. She has provided me with endless support. She helped me with the content and editing of this book. She has been a constant source of encouragement and inspiration. I love you Bhavna.

REGISTER THIS BOOK FOR FREEBIES

TO GET FREE UPDATES AND FREE VIDEOS

To get updates to this book and access to free videos that will show you how to further enhance your relationship with God through hearing His Voice, please visit:

www.destined4torah.com/registerbook

WHY DID I WRITE THIS BOOK?

I wrote this book because I desire that everyone learns how to hear the Voice of God. I have a burning desire to draw people into the depths of the Torah. I use the words, Bible and Torah interchangeably. The Bible teaches you how to hear the Voice of God. The Bible is not dead history. It is living. The writer of Hebrews tells us:

[HEBREWS 4:12 KJV] "12 FOR THE WORD OF GOD [IS] QUICK, AND POWERFUL, AND SHARPER THAN ANY TWOEDGED SWORD, PIERCING EVEN TO THE DIVIDING ASUNDER OF SOUL AND SPIRIT, AND OF THE JOINTS AND MARROW, AND [IS] A DISCERNER OF THE THOUGHTS AND INTENTS OF THE HEART."

I learned to hear the Voice of God through the most painful events of my life. It is often through the pain and desperation that the Lord reveals Himself to you. It is my prayer that the Lord will reveal Himself to you as you read this book. I encourage you to use this book as a guide to help you in your personal journey. It is my passion that you look into the Torah, the Living Word of

God and discover God's design for your destiny through His Voice.

WHY SHOULD YOU READ THIS BOOK?

This book will help you to discern God's will for your life. Within the pages of this book, you will learn about some of the great figures in the Bible and how they learned how to follow the Lord in every aspect of their lives through His Voice.

Imagine the Lord directing every major event and even every footstep in your life. This book will inspire you to trust the Lord in everything. You can expect the Lord to direct every event of your life through His Voice. This book will show you the process. Trust the process.

Your life is as much spiritual as it is physical. The Torah provides the blueprint for every area of your life. Allow me to take you on a journey to hearing His Voice. He is always speaking. I invite you to allow the Lord to open your eyes and ears to hearing His Voice.

"THE TORAH IS NOT JUST A COMPENDIUM OF BIBLE STORIES. RATHER, IT IS A BOOK OF LIFE AUTHORED BY GOD HIMSELF. EVERY WORD, EVERY LETTER, EVERY PUNCTUATION MARK IS LADEN WITH HIDDEN MEANING — ALL DESIGNED TO ENSURE A MEANINGFUL AND BLESSED JOURNEY ON THIS PLANET. THEREFORE, WE ASK THAT GOD OPEN OUR EYES, OUR MINDS, AND OUR HEARTS TO THE DIVINE WISDOM CONCEALED IN HIS SACRED WORDS."[1]

CHAPTER 1 – THE VOICE OF GOD

[PSALM 139:7-10 KJV] "7 WHITHER SHALL I GO FROM THY SPIRIT? OR WHITHER SHALL I FLEE FROM THY PRESENCE? 8 IF I ASCEND UP INTO HEAVEN, THOU [ART] THERE: IF I MAKE MY BED IN HELL, BEHOLD, THOU [ART THERE]. 9 [IF] I TAKE THE WINGS OF THE MORNING, [AND] DWELL IN THE UTTERMOST PARTS OF THE SEA; 10 EVEN THERE SHALL THY HAND LEAD ME, AND THY RIGHT HAND SHALL HOLD ME."

IMAGINE

Can you imagine having the ability to hear the audible Voice of God. The purpose of this book is to teach you how to hear God's Voice. Many biblical figures heard the audible voice of God including Adam, Eve, Abraham, Moses, the Israelites that stood at the foot of Mount Sinai at the giving of the Torah, Samuel, Elijah, our Lord and Savior Jesus, and the apostles. This list is not an all and inclusive list of those that heard God's audible Voice, but these names provide a good sample. It is my hope that you use this book to assist you in your personal journey to hear God's Voice. Let's not limit God's Voice to only an audible experience. God is always speaking through His wondrous creation. It is my sincere desire that you come to hear God's Voice in the Earth, Wind, Fire & a Still Small Voice. He also speaks to us in the Biblical Feasts which are times in which God manifests His Presence in magnificent ways. I invite you to make this journey personal. The Lord desires to speak to you.

GOD'S VOICE IS EVERYWHERE

There is nowhere we can go to hide from God's Presence. God is always speaking. God's voice does not dissipate the way our voices dissipate into echoes. God's voice doesn't echo because it is not reflected back by any material. At Mount Sinai, God's voice was absorbed by the mountains. Adam and Eve tried to hide and failed. Jonah ran away from God's voice and ended up being swallowed by a whale that carried him free of charge to his final destination, Nineveh. We will talk about Jonah later. Even Elijah tried to run away from God's voice when he fled from Jezebel. Elijah had such an amazing relationship with God that there was no place in His life that was void of

God's voice. In this book, we will use the words, "God's moving," "God's Voice" and "God's Presence" interchangeably.

Elijah was probably more accustomed with the moves of the Spirit of God than any other prophet in the Hebrew Scriptures. After he destroyed the prophets of Baal, he fled from Jezebel to Mount Sinai. He encountered the Lord and the Lord asked him the question: "What are you doing here?

WHAT ARE YOU DOING HERE?

[1 KINGS 19:9 KJV] "9 AND HE CAME THITHER UNTO A CAVE, AND LODGED THERE; AND, BEHOLD, THE WORD OF THE LORD [CAME] TO HIM, AND HE SAID UNTO HIM, WHAT DOEST THOU HERE, ELIJAH? "

Does this question sound familiar? Where else have you heard of God asking man a question? It first happened in the Garden of Eden after Adam and Eve ate of the forbidden fruit of the tree of the knowledge of good and evil:

[GENESIS 3:9 KJV] "9 AND THE LORD GOD CALLED UNTO ADAM, AND SAID UNTO HIM, WHERE [ART] THOU?"

Why would the Lord even ask questions when he already knows everything? This is one of His incommunicable attributes. God has many incommunicable attributes. Incommunicable attributes are attributes that belong to God alone and that cannot be shared with mankind and not even with the angels in heaven. Three of these attributes are God's omnipresence, omnipotence, and omniscience. God's omnipresence refers to Him being present everywhere. God's omnipotence refers to Him being all powerful. God's omniscience refers to Him knowing everything. In the above scriptures, we see God's omniscience in action. God already knew that Adam and Eve had eaten of the forbidden knowledge of good and evil. The reason why God asked this question was because He wanted to restore the relationship that Adam and Eve once had with God. He asked Adam the question because He wanted to lead him on the path of teshuva (repentance). He wanted Adam and Eve to take ownership for the sin they had committed. Instead of taking ownership, Adam blamed Eve, and Eve in turn blamed the Serpent. One of the most difficult things for people to do is to take ownership for their faults. Most of us struggle with taking ownership for our faults. I believe that if Adam and Eve would have acknowledged their sin, taken ownership for their disobedience, and repented, then God would have restored them. Because of their lack of repentance, God exiled mankind from the Garden of Eden. Mankind has lived in exile ever since. This is a lesson that you can apply to your lives on a daily basis. This is a question that the Lord is going to ask you whenever you deviate away from His commandments.

You may see how the question of "Where are you?" relates to Adam and Eve but what does it have to do with Elijah? What did Elijah do wrong? The answer to this question isn't so obvious. Let's dig into the text.

[1 KINGS 19:9-13 KJV] "9 AND HE CAME
THITHER UNTO A CAVE, AND LODGED THERE;
AND, BEHOLD, THE WORD OF THE LORD [CAME]
TO HIM, AND HE SAID UNTO HIM, WHAT DOEST
THOU HERE, ELIJAH? 10 AND HE SAID, I HAVE
BEEN VERY JEALOUS FOR THE LORD GOD OF
HOSTS: FOR THE CHILDREN OF ISRAEL HAVE
FORSAKEN THY COVENANT, THROWN DOWN THINE
ALTARS, AND SLAIN THY PROPHETS WITH THE
SWORD; AND I, [EVEN] I ONLY, AM LEFT; AND
THEY SEEK MY LIFE, TO TAKE IT AWAY. 11 AND HE
SAID, GO FORTH, AND STAND UPON THE MOUNT
BEFORE THE LORD. AND, BEHOLD, THE LORD
PASSED BY, AND A GREAT AND STRONG WIND RENT
THE MOUNTAINS, AND BRAKE IN PIECES THE
ROCKS BEFORE THE LORD; [BUT] THE LORD
[WAS] NOT IN THE WIND: AND AFTER THE WIND
AN EARTHQUAKE; [BUT] THE LORD [WAS] NOT
IN THE EARTHQUAKE: 12 AND AFTER THE
EARTHQUAKE A FIRE; [BUT] THE LORD [WAS]
NOT IN THE FIRE: AND AFTER THE FIRE A STILL
SMALL VOICE. 13 AND IT WAS [SO], WHEN ELIJAH
HEARD [IT], THAT HE WRAPPED HIS FACE IN HIS
MANTLE, AND WENT OUT, AND STOOD IN THE
ENTERING IN OF THE CAVE. AND, BEHOLD,

*[THERE CAME] A VOICE UNTO HIM, AND SAID,
WHAT DOEST THOU HERE, ELIJAH?"*

Elijah was so familiar with the moving of the
Spirit of God. Elijah was so sensitive to the Holy
Spirit that He discerned when He was present.
In his ministry, he encountered the Holy Spirit
in the earth, in the wind, and in the fire. He was
also sensitive enough to recognize when the
Holy Spirit was not present. For example, he
discerned that the Holy Spirit was not present in
the wind in 1 Kings 19. There is a teaching here
for us. We should be so sensitive to the Holy
Spirit that we can discern when He is present
and when He is not present. Sometimes we can
be so accustomed to the supernatural that we
forget about the Person behind the supernatural.
We should be so sensitive to the Holy Spirit that
we can discern when it is Him and not be lead
astray by an imitation. Elijah then received a
new revelation of the Holy Spirit in the "Still,
Small Voice." I believe this is the highest
manifestation of God's Presence that we can
encounter in life. You are going to learn about
the manifestations of the Holy Spirit in the earth,
wind, fire, and finally in the "Still, Small Voice."
Imagine feeling the Presence of God so much
that every fiber of your being is consumed with
the Holy Spirit. As you read this book, you may
find yourself entering into a new relationship
with the Holy Spirit. This book is not just about

25

encountering the Holy Spirit through the open demonstrations of His miraculous power. This book is also about getting to know the Holy Spirit in the most intimate ways. This book is about relationship with the Lord. Let's get to know Him together. Moses knew His ways. Knowing His ways is to know Him.

> *[DEUTERONOMY 34:10 KJV] "10 AND THERE AROSE NOT A PROPHET SINCE IN ISRAEL LIKE UNTO MOSES, WHOM THE LORD KNEW FACE TO FACE,"*

> *[PSALM 103:7 KJV] "7 HE MADE KNOWN HIS WAYS UNTO MOSES, HIS ACTS UNTO THE CHILDREN OF ISRAEL."*

Knowing His ways means that we stay in relationship with Him. Our relationship with God should be continual and not something you only experience during holy days. What would your spouse think if you both only visited on birthdays and anniversaries? It sounds ludicrous, doesn't it? How much more does it apply to our relationship with our Heavenly Spouse.

MOVED BY THE SPIRIT OF GOD

[GENESIS 1:2 KJV] "2 AND THE EARTH WAS WITHOUT FORM, AND VOID; AND DARKNESS [WAS] UPON THE FACE OF THE DEEP. AND THE SPIRIT OF GOD MOVED UPON THE FACE OF THE WATERS."

The Spirit of God is about to move upon your destiny in the most peculiar way. He will disrupt the mundane in your life. He will challenge your prejudices and beliefs. He will convict you of sin. He will mold you into the image that He designed for you. He will bring you a mighty revelation of God and a burden for souls like you have never experienced. I am going to teach you about encounters with God that will change your lives forever. Who is the Spirit of God? The Spirit of God is not an "it." But rather, He is a Person. He is the 3rd Person of the Trinity. His Name is The Holy Spirit or the Ruach HaKadosh. I would like to introduce Him to you throughout the Torah.

In my previous book, The Final Countdown, I introduced you to the Hebrew Aleph-Beit. The Hebrew Aleph-Beit is not an alphabet like the

English alphabet composed of letters that are used to build words and sentences. An English word for an object is just a label. In Hebrew, the word for an object is much more than a label. It is living and breathing. The word defines the essence of the creature. It defines the destiny of the creature. The Holy Spirit will not act or move without a substance to act upon. What is that substance? That substance is the Word of God. Without the Word of God, your life is void.'

THE WORD OF GOD COMES

ISAIAH 55:11 (KJV) "11 SO SHALL MY WORD BE THAT GOETH FORTH OUT OF MY MOUTH: IT SHALL NOT RETURN UNTO ME VOID, BUT IT SHALL ACCOMPLISH THAT WHICH I PLEASE, AND IT SHALL PROSPER [IN THE THING] WHERETO I SENT IT."

1 PETER 1:25 (KJV) "25 BUT THE WORD OF THE LORD ENDURETH FOR EVER. AND THIS IS THE WORD WHICH BY THE GOSPEL IS PREACHED UNTO YOU."

2 THESSALONIANS 3:1 (KJV) "1 FINALLY, BRETHREN, PRAY FOR US, THAT THE WORD OF THE LORD MAY HAVE [FREE] COURSE, AND BE GLORIFIED, EVEN AS [IT IS] WITH YOU:"

1 THESSALONIANS 1:8 (KJV) "8 FOR FROM YOU SOUNDED OUT THE WORD OF THE LORD NOT ONLY IN MACEDONIA AND ACHAIA, BUT ALSO IN EVERY PLACE YOUR FAITH TO GOD-WARD IS SPREAD ABROAD; SO THAT WE NEED NOT TO SPEAK ANY THING."

1 THESSALONIANS 1:6 (KJV) "6 AND YE BECAME FOLLOWERS OF US, AND OF THE LORD, HAVING RECEIVED THE WORD IN MUCH AFFLICTION, WITH JOY OF THE HOLY GHOST:"

God's word is always moving. In fact, God's word is what keeps all of creation in existence. He upholds everything by the power of His Word. The more of the word that is in you, the more you will experience the moving of the Spirit of God in your life. The Spirit of God needs substance to move upon. That substance is the word of God. In fact, the Spirit of God did not create the universe from nothing. That is what we are often taught. He created the universe using the letters of the Hebrew alphabet (Aleph-Beit). See Chapter 3 Your Substance from my book, The Final Countdown for a detailed explanation.

THE THREE ERAS OF HUMAN HISTORY

There are three periods in human history that are divided into three 2,000-year periods. The three eras demonstrate the different ways in which the Voice of God moved upon the earth.

[GENESIS 1:2 KJV] "2 AND THE EARTH WAS WITHOUT FORM, AND VOID; AND DARKNESS [WAS] UPON THE FACE OF THE DEEP. AND THE SPIRIT OF GOD MOVED UPON THE FACE OF THE WATERS."

The first period is known as the period of the Void or Tohu. This began with the fall of Adam and Eve when they were exiled from the Garden of Eden. This was a period without the teachings of Torah and without a longing for God. This period of the Void was a period of distance from God.

[GENESIS 12:1 KJV] "1 NOW THE LORD HAD SAID UNTO ABRAM, GET THEE OUT OF THY COUNTRY, AND FROM THY KINDRED, AND FROM

THY FATHER'S HOUSE, UNTO A LAND THAT I WILL SHEW THEE:"

The second 2,000-year period began when Abram was born in the Hebrew year 1948. This is not 1948 AD. The Hebrew year 1948 is 1,948 years since the creation of Adam. At the time I wrote this book, we were in the Hebrew year 5778. Abram and his wife, Sarai reintroduced Monotheism, the belief in one God, into the world. I would call them the first missionaries in the world. They converted souls wherever they went. Abram converted and taught the men and Sarai converted and taught the women.

[MATTHEW 1:23 KJV] "23 BEHOLD, A VIRGIN SHALL BE WITH CHILD, AND SHALL BRING FORTH A SON, AND THEY SHALL CALL HIS NAME EMMANUEL, WHICH BEING INTERPRETED IS, GOD WITH US."

The third 2,000-year period began roughly 2,000 years ago when Jesus was born in Bethlehem. This period will come to an end when King Mashiach, Jesus returns and ushers in His millennial reign. His millennial reign corresponds to the 7th Day of Creation.

These three 2,000-year periods reveal the different ways in which God reveals His Voice in creation. The ultimate goal of God's Voice is to bring the creation into perfection:

[ROMANS 8:22-23 KJV] "22 FOR WE KNOW THAT THE WHOLE CREATION GROANETH AND TRAVAILETH IN PAIN TOGETHER UNTIL NOW. 23 AND NOT ONLY [THEY], BUT OURSELVES ALSO, WHICH HAVE THE FIRSTFRUITS OF THE SPIRIT, EVEN WE OURSELVES GROAN WITHIN OURSELVES, WAITING FOR THE ADOPTION, [TO WIT], THE REDEMPTION OF OUR BODY."

We are in the final 2,000-year period which will be complete with the Messiah's return. God is perfecting us for the Messiah's return. God is speaking to us through the groaning that will bring us to perfection. I will elaborate on this concept in my next book, Your Final Destination. In this final 2,000 year period, God is speaking to His creation and calling all of us to repentance and salvation. God also speaks to us in the Feasts of the Lord.

THE FEASTS OF THE LORD

[LEVITICUS 23:4-5, 16, 24, 27, 34, 37 KJV] "4 THESE [ARE] THE FEASTS OF THE LORD, [EVEN] HOLY CONVOCATIONS, WHICH YE SHALL PROCLAIM IN THEIR SEASONS. 5 IN THE FOURTEENTH [DAY] OF THE FIRST MONTH AT EVEN [IS] THE LORD'S PASSOVER. ... 16 EVEN UNTO THE MORROW AFTER THE SEVENTH SABBATH SHALL YE NUMBER FIFTY DAYS; AND YE SHALL OFFER A NEW MEAT OFFERING UNTO THE LORD. ... 24 SPEAK UNTO THE CHILDREN OF ISRAEL, SAYING, IN THE SEVENTH MONTH, IN THE FIRST [DAY] OF THE MONTH, SHALL YE HAVE A SABBATH, A MEMORIAL OF BLOWING OF TRUMPETS, AN HOLY CONVOCATION. ... 27 ALSO ON THE TENTH [DAY] OF THIS SEVENTH MONTH [THERE SHALL BE] A DAY OF ATONEMENT: IT SHALL BE AN HOLY CONVOCATION UNTO YOU; AND YE SHALL AFFLICT YOUR SOULS, AND OFFER AN OFFERING MADE BY FIRE UNTO THE LORD. ... 34 SPEAK UNTO THE CHILDREN OF ISRAEL, SAYING, THE FIFTEENTH DAY OF THIS SEVENTH MONTH [SHALL BE] THE FEAST OF TABERNACLES

[FOR] SEVEN DAYS UNTO THE LORD. ... 37
THESE [ARE] THE FEASTS OF THE LORD, WHICH
YE SHALL PROCLAIM [TO BE] HOLY
CONVOCATIONS, TO OFFER AN OFFERING MADE
BY FIRE UNTO THE LORD, A BURNT OFFERING,
AND A MEAT OFFERING, A SACRIFICE, AND DRINK
OFFERINGS, EVERY THING UPON HIS DAY:"

We see many major moves of the Holy Spirit
that occur on Biblical feasts. God speaks to us in
His feasts. One of the greatest ways you can
know the voice of the Holy Spirit is by studying
the feasts of the Lord. I would like to explain to
you what the Biblical feasts are. Moses
introduces us to the feasts and high holidays in
Leviticus 23. Every major event in Jesus'
ministry occurred during a feast.

These feasts and high holy days include Pesach
(Passover) in verse 5 above, Shavuot (Pentecost)
in verse 6, Rosh Hashanah (Jewish New Year) in
verse 24, Yom Kippur (Day of Atonement) in
verse 27, and Sukkot (The Feast of Tabernacles)
in verse 34. These days are days in which God
designed to meet with His people in a
supernatural way. These are not just gatherings
for special occasions. These are days filled with
God's anointing. The Lord wants you to

experience the fullness of these Divine encounters with God during the feasts of the Lord.

There are three main Shalosh Regalim (Pilgrimage Feasts) in which ancient Jewish men were commanded to appear before God in Jerusalem:

1. Pesach (Passover or Unleavened Bread)

2. Shavuot (1st Fruits, Feast of Weeks or Pentecost)

3. Sukkot (Ingathering, Feast of Tabernacles)

In addition to the 3 main festivals, the Jews also have minor feasts including Chanukah (Hannukah) and Purim. These are not the major feasts that were instituted by Moses. These minor feasts were instituted by the Rabbis.

[GENESIS 1:1 KJV] "1 IN THE BEGINNING GOD CREATED THE HEAVEN AND THE EARTH."

You may not know this. The Hebrew New Year wasn't first introduced by Moses in Leviticus 23. It was first introduced by Moses in Genesis 1:1. Moses was the author of the Torah, Genesis through Deuteronomy. Unlike the Gregorian calendar in which New Year's Day is celebrated on the first day of the first month of the year, the Jewish New Year is celebrated on the first day of the seventh month. If you are not confused already, then please allow me to confuse you a little more. Just joking! I will clarify. The Hebrew day doesn't begin at midnight. The Hebrew day begins at sunset as you read throughout Genesis 1, "And the evening and the morning were the … day." The date on the Hebrew calendar increments at sunset rather than midnight as we are accustomed to. During the first Rosh Hashanah, the Spirit of God moved upon the face of the waters. He has not stopped moving upon the face of the waters. The waters represent the Word of God. Whenever the word is spoken, the Spirit of God is moving. The Rabbis tells us that God created the Heavens and Earth on Rosh Hashanah. They prophetically received this revelation by rearranging the letters of the first three words in the Bible, "In the beginning." Let's play rabbinic scrabble. By rearranging the letters of the words, "In the beginning" in Hebrew, it can read, "On the first of Tishrei." I may have stirred up a couple questions. What is Tishrei? What does that have to do with Rosh Hashanah?

Allow me to explain. It has everything to do with it. Tishrei is the seventh month of the Hebrew calendar. The 1st day of Tishrei is the Hebrew New Year which is called Rosh Hashanah. The Sages have discovered that God embedded a secret code in Genesis 1:1. They discovered that God created the heavens and the earth on Rosh Hashanah.

Genesis 1:1 can also read: "On the first of Tishrei, God created the heaven and the earth." Only the Holy Spirit can embed such a prophetic revelation in the Bible. You still may be a little confused. You may ask, "why do you call the first day of the seventh month, Rosh Hashanah? Shouldn't the first day of the first month be Rosh Hashanah?" It's easy to confuse secular concepts with biblical concepts. On the biblical calendar, the first day of the seventh month is the Hebrew New Year. On our secular calendar, the first day of the first month of the year is New Year's Day. There is nothing prophetic about the secular New Year's Day, January 1. The Biblical New Year's Day is full of the power of God.

Many of us have extracted the Jewishness out of the Bible in both the Tanakh and in the New Testament. It's like we have taken a medical syringe with a needle and removed the Jewishness out of the Bible. None of the prophets including Moses gave up their Jewish identities. In fact, Jesus never gave up His Jewish identity. He was born, died, and resurrected as a Jew. Even the Apostles never gave up their Jewish identities. Then why do we remove the Jewishness out of the Word of God? Often when we study the Bible, we study it from our cultural and historical context. We need to apply Biblical truths into the contexts of our lives but we need to study it within its Jewish context. When the prophets of old wrote the books of the Bible, they wrote the word under the inspiration of the Holy Spirit. These words were written down for all generations. The Bible is timeless. That means that the Bible is just as relevant to the people that lived in the 1st century as it is to us that live in the 21st century. Many of the words of scripture include Biblical feasts. Let's now take our syringes and needles and reinsert Jewishness into the Bible. I want you to experience all that God has for you. All that God has for you includes the Biblical feasts. Are you ready for the Holy Spirit to move upon your life?

[MARK 1:41 KJV] "41 AND JESUS, MOVED WITH COMPASSION, PUT FORTH [HIS] HAND, AND TOUCHED HIM, AND SAITH UNTO HIM, I WILL; BE THOU CLEAN."

[MARK 6:34 KJV] "34 AND JESUS, WHEN HE CAME OUT, SAW MUCH PEOPLE, AND WAS MOVED WITH COMPASSION TOWARD THEM, BECAUSE THEY WERE AS SHEEP NOT HAVING A SHEPHERD: AND HE BEGAN TO TEACH THEM MANY THINGS."

Jesus, who was so filled with the Spirit of God, was moved with compassion for His people. Just as the Spirit of God moved upon the waters, Jesus was moved with compassion for His people. You will learn keys to help you be moved by the Spirit of God.

[2 PETER 1:21 KJV] "21 FOR THE PROPHECY CAME NOT IN OLD TIME BY THE WILL OF MAN: BUT HOLY MEN OF GOD SPAKE [AS THEY WERE] MOVED BY THE HOLY GHOST."

When the prophets of the Hebrew Scriptures were moved by the Spirit of God, they spoke and wrote prophetically.

The Spirit of God is also moving upon the face of your waters. The more of the Word of God is in you, then the more the Spirit of God is going to move upon you. He is looking for pliable vessels that He can mold and use for His glory. No flesh can glory in His Presence. In fact, being full of self will void His Presence in your life. The Rabbis teach us that when one's heart is full of arrogance, there is no room for God.

ROSH HASHANAH - ON A DAY

[GENESIS 1:1 KJV] "1 IN THE BEGINNING GOD CREATED THE HEAVEN AND THE EARTH."

We see the first move of the Holy Spirit in Genesis 1:2. He moves upon the face of the waters. Many of the mighty moves of the Holy Spirit occur during the Hebrew feasts. For example, the first might move of the Holy Spirit began on Rosh Hashanah. Let's look at events that occurred on Rosh Hashanah. The heavens and the earth were created on the first Rosh Hashanah. Many other events occurred on Rosh Hashanah.

[GENESIS 1:27 KJV] "27 SO GOD CREATED MAN IN HIS [OWN] IMAGE, IN THE IMAGE OF GOD CREATED HE HIM; MALE AND FEMALE CREATED HE THEM."

Man was created on Rosh Hashanah. Both Adam and Eve were created on Rosh Hashanah.

[GENESIS 2:15 KJV] "15 AND THE LORD GOD TOOK THE MAN, AND PUT HIM INTO THE GARDEN OF EDEN TO DRESS IT AND TO KEEP IT."

Adam was placed into priestly service in the Garden on a Rosh Hashanah. The "dressing and keeping" was some form of priestly service. I believe Adam was a type of gatekeeper to the world.

[GENESIS 18:10, 14 KJV] "10 AND HE SAID, I WILL CERTAINLY RETURN UNTO THEE ACCORDING TO THE TIME OF LIFE; AND, LO, SARAH THY WIFE SHALL HAVE A SON. AND SARAH HEARD [IT] IN THE TENT DOOR, WHICH [WAS] BEHIND HIM. ... 14 IS ANY THING TOO HARD FOR THE LORD? AT THE TIME APPOINTED I WILL RETURN UNTO THEE, ACCORDING TO THE TIME OF LIFE, AND SARAH SHALL HAVE A SON."

The Lord visited Sarah on a Rosh Hashanah. She conceived her son, Isaac on Rosh Hashanah. She was 89 years old and her husband, Abraham was 99 years old when they received this word.

GENESIS 21:1-3 KJV] "1 AND THE LORD VISITED SARAH AS HE HAD SAID, AND THE LORD DID UNTO SARAH AS HE HAD SPOKEN. 2 FOR SARAH CONCEIVED, AND BARE ABRAHAM A SON IN HIS OLD AGE, AT THE SET TIME OF WHICH GOD HAD SPOKEN TO HIM. 3 AND ABRAHAM CALLED THE NAME OF HIS SON THAT WAS BORN UNTO HIM, WHOM SARAH BARE TO HIM, ISAAC."

[GENESIS 41:9, KJV] "9 THEN SPAKE THE CHIEF BUTLER UNTO PHARAOH, SAYING, I DO REMEMBER MY FAULTS THIS DAY: ... "

The butler remembered the goodness that Joseph showed him. A few years earlier, while both Joseph and Pharaoh's butler were in prison, Joseph interpreted the butler's troubling dream. Joseph interpreted that the butler would be restored to his prominent position as the king's chief butler within 3 days. Joseph in turn asked the butler to remember him when he returns to his position. This is where I believe Joseph made a mistake. Instead of relying upon

God to release him from prison, he asked the chief butler to remember him when he returns to his position.

[GENESIS 40:23 KJV] "23 YET DID NOT THE CHIEF BUTLER REMEMBER JOSEPH, BUT FORGAT HIM."

Because of this error in judgment, the Lord extended his time in prison another 2 years. It's not man that is going to remember you. It is God who is going to remember you for good on Rosh Hashanah.

[GENESIS 41:14, 25, 29-30, 32, 39-42 KJV] "14 THEN PHARAOH SENT AND CALLED JOSEPH, AND THEY BROUGHT HIM HASTILY OUT OF THE DUNGEON: AND HE SHAVED [HIMSELF], AND CHANGED HIS RAIMENT, AND CAME IN UNTO PHARAOH. ... 25 AND JOSEPH SAID UNTO PHARAOH, THE DREAM OF PHARAOH [IS] ONE: GOD HATH SHEWED PHARAOH WHAT HE [IS] ABOUT TO DO. ... 29 BEHOLD, THERE COME

SEVEN YEARS OF GREAT PLENTY THROUGHOUT ALL THE LAND OF EGYPT: 30 AND THERE SHALL ARISE AFTER THEM SEVEN YEARS OF FAMINE; AND ALL THE PLENTY SHALL BE FORGOTTEN IN THE LAND OF EGYPT; AND THE FAMINE SHALL CONSUME THE LAND; ... 32 AND FOR THAT THE DREAM WAS DOUBLED UNTO PHARAOH TWICE; [IT IS] BECAUSE THE THING [IS] ESTABLISHED BY GOD, AND GOD WILL SHORTLY BRING IT TO PASS. ... 39 AND PHARAOH SAID UNTO JOSEPH, FORASMUCH AS GOD HATH SHEWED THEE ALL THIS, [THERE IS] NONE SO DISCREET AND WISE AS THOU [ART]: 40 THOU SHALT BE OVER MY HOUSE, AND ACCORDING UNTO THY WORD SHALL ALL MY PEOPLE BE RULED: ONLY IN THE THRONE WILL I BE GREATER THAN THOU. 41 AND PHARAOH SAID UNTO JOSEPH, SEE, I HAVE SET THEE OVER ALL THE LAND OF EGYPT. 42 AND PHARAOH TOOK OFF HIS RING FROM HIS HAND, AND PUT IT UPON JOSEPH'S HAND, AND ARRAYED HIM IN VESTURES OF FINE LINEN, AND PUT A GOLD CHAIN ABOUT HIS NECK;"

Joseph came out of prison, interpreted Pharaoh's dreams, and was crowned viceroy of Egypt on

Rosh Hashanah. He was second only to
Pharaoh.

*[1 SAMUEL 1:11, 20 KJV] "11 AND SHE VOWED A
VOW, AND SAID, O LORD OF HOSTS, IF THOU
WILT INDEED LOOK ON THE AFFLICTION OF THINE
HANDMAID, AND REMEMBER ME, AND NOT
FORGET THINE HANDMAID, BUT WILT GIVE UNTO
THINE HANDMAID A MAN CHILD, THEN I WILL
GIVE HIM UNTO THE LORD ALL THE DAYS OF HIS
LIFE, AND THERE SHALL NO RAZOR COME UPON
HIS HEAD. ... 20 WHEREFORE IT CAME TO PASS,
WHEN THE TIME WAS COME ABOUT AFTER
HANNAH HAD CONCEIVED, THAT SHE BARE A SON,
AND CALLED HIS NAME SAMUEL, [SAYING],
BECAUSE I HAVE ASKED HIM OF THE LORD."*

Hannah conceived on Rosh Hashanah. The
Midrash states that Hannah became pregnant on
Rosh Hashanah, because the Bible says of her (v.
19) "and the Lord remembered her" and Rosh
Hashanah is called (Lev. 23:24) "a sacred
occasion commemorated [zikhron] with loud
blasts"

Hannah was one hundred and thirty years old when she became pregnant with Samuel. Do you know who else was 130 years old when she became pregnant? Jochebed, the mother of Moses was also hundred and thirty years old when she became pregnant with Moses.

[2 KINGS 4:11-13 KJV] "11 AND IT FELL ON A DAY, THAT HE CAME THITHER, AND HE TURNED INTO THE CHAMBER, AND LAY THERE. 12 AND HE SAID TO GEHAZI HIS SERVANT, CALL THIS SHUNAMMITE. AND WHEN HE HAD CALLED HER, SHE STOOD BEFORE HIM. 13 AND HE SAID UNTO HIM, SAY NOW UNTO HER, BEHOLD, THOU HAST BEEN CAREFUL FOR US WITH ALL THIS CARE; WHAT [IS] TO BE DONE FOR THEE? WOULDEST THOU BE SPOKEN FOR TO THE KING, OR TO THE CAPTAIN OF THE HOST? AND SHE ANSWERED, I DWELL AMONG MINE OWN PEOPLE."

[2 KINGS 4:14-16 KJV] "14 AND HE SAID, WHAT THEN [IS] TO BE DONE FOR HER? AND GEHAZI ANSWERED, VERILY SHE HATH NO CHILD, AND HER HUSBAND IS OLD. 15 AND HE SAID, CALL

HER. AND WHEN HE HAD CALLED HER, SHE STOOD IN THE DOOR. 16 AND HE SAID, ABOUT THIS SEASON, ACCORDING TO THE TIME OF LIFE, THOU SHALT EMBRACE A SON. AND SHE SAID, NAY, MY LORD, [THOU] MAN OF GOD, DO NOT LIE UNTO THINE HANDMAID."

The prophetic word came to the Shunammite woman on Rosh Hashanah - "Wouldest thou be spoken for to the King of heaven today?" She was the greatest woman of her time. She was as God fearing as the Matriarchs Sarah and Rebecca. Some say she was the sister of Abishag, the Shunammite woman who attended David at the end of his life (1 Kings 1:3). Some say she was the wife or mother of the prophet Iddo. She became the mother of the prophet, Habbakuk.

[REVELATION 1:10 KJV] "10 I WAS IN THE SPIRIT ON THE LORD'S DAY, AND HEARD BEHIND ME A GREAT VOICE, AS OF A TRUMPET,"

And finally, the book of Revelation begins on Rosh Hashanah. Why "A Day?" Let's return to Genesis 1. In the description of the story of creation, there is an interesting anomaly in the words used. After the first day of creation, the Torah says, "It was evening it was day, one day."

BEREISHIT 1:5 "AND GOD CALLED THE LIGHT DAY, AND THE DARKNESS HE CALLED NIGHT, AND IT WAS EVENING AND IT WAS MORNING, ONE DAY."[ii]

In the successive days, days 2 through 7, "It was evening it was, the second day... third day... fourth day... etc." Following this sequence, after the first day the Torah should logically have said, "It was evening it was day, the first day." Why "one day?" From this statement, the Rabbinic Sages infer that the first day was a day of oneness in which God was alone. Only God was present. All of His angels were created on the following day.

PESACH

*[EXODUS 12:23 KJV] "23 FOR THE LORD WILL
PASS THROUGH TO SMITE THE EGYPTIANS; AND
WHEN HE SEETH THE BLOOD UPON THE LINTEL,
AND ON THE TWO SIDE POSTS, THE LORD WILL
PASS OVER THE DOOR, AND WILL NOT SUFFER THE
DESTROYER TO COME IN UNTO YOUR HOUSES TO
SMITE [YOU]."*

Remember that I told you that most major
moves of the Holy Spirit occurred on a Biblical
Feast. On Pesach, when the Israelites were
taken out of Egypt, they became designated as
God's agents to the world. Passover teaches us
to remember the miracles which God performed
in Egypt, and to perpetuate their memory. We
don't just perpetuate the memory, we also
experience the deliverance in our lives. During
Passover, the Israelites were protected from the
plague of the killing of all the firstborn by the
blood on the doorposts. The spirit of death
passed over the homes that had the blood of the
lambs on their doorposts. Thus, we get the
name Passover or Pesach for the feast. The
Israelites were taken out of the bondage of the
Egyptians during Passover. The Hebrew word

for Egyptians is Mitzrayim. Mitzrayim means restrictions or narrow place. Every year during Passover, we experience deliverance from restrictions in our lives. Jesus was crucified and resurrected on Pesach.

On Pesach, when the Israelites were taken out of Egypt, they became designated as God's agents to the world. It was also during a Pesach, nearly 2,000 years ago that Jesus commissioned the Apostles to take the gospel to the nations:

[MATTHEW 28:19 KJV] "19 GO YE THEREFORE, AND TEACH ALL NATIONS, BAPTIZING THEM IN THE NAME OF THE FATHER, AND OF THE SON, AND OF THE HOLY GHOST:"

[PERKEI AVOT 6:10] "G-D ACQUIRED FIVE ACQUISITIONS IN HIS WORLD. THESE ARE: ONE ACQUISITION IS THE TORAH, ONE ACQUISITION ARE THE HEAVENS AND THE EARTH, ONE ACQUISITION IS ABRAHAM, ONE ACQUISITION IS THE PEOPLE OF ISRAEL, AND ONE ACQUISITION IS THE HOLY TEMPLE. THE TORAH, AS IT IS WRITTEN (PROVERBS 8:22), "G-D ACQUIRED ME AS THE BEGINNING OF HIS WAY, BEFORE HIS WORKS OF YORE." THE HEAVENS AND THE EARTH, AS IT IS WRITTEN (ISAIAH 66:1), "SO SAYS G-D: THE HEAVENS ARE MY THRONE AND THE EARTH IS MY FOOTSTOOL; WHAT HOUSE, THEN, CAN YOU BUILD FOR ME, AND WHERE IS MY PLACE OF REST?"; AND IT SAYS (PSALMS 104:25), "HOW MANY ARE YOUR WORKS, O G-D, YOU HAVE MADE THEM ALL WITH WISDOM; THE EARTH IS FILLED WITH YOUR ACQUISITIONS." ABRAHAM, AS IT IS WRITTEN (GENESIS 14:19), "AND HE BLESSED HIM, AND SAID: BLESSED BE ABRAM TO G-D MOST HIGH, ACQUIRER OF HEAVENS AND EARTH." ISRAEL, AS IT IS WRITTEN (EXODUS 15:16), "TILL YOUR NATION, O G-D, SHALL PASS, TILL THIS NATION YOU HAVE ACQUIRED SHALL PASS"; AND IT SAYS (PSALMS 16:3), "TO THE HOLY WHO ARE UPON

EARTH, THE NOBLE ONES, IN WHOM IS ALL MY DELIGHT." THE HOLY TEMPLE, AS IT IS WRITTEN (EXODUS 15:17), "THE BASE FOR YOUR DWELLING THAT YOU, G-D, HAVE ACHIEVED; THE SANCTUARY, O L-RD, THAT YOUR HANDS HAVE ESTABLISHED"; AND IT SAYS (PSALMS 78:54), "AND HE BROUGHT THEM TO HIS HOLY DOMAIN, THIS MOUNT HIS RIGHT HAND HAS ACQUIRED.""

CHAPTER 2 – EARTH

ADAM'S DESTINY

[GENESIS 2:15 KJV] "AND THE LORD GOD TOOK THE MAN, AND PUT HIM INTO THE GARDEN OF EDEN TO DRESS IT AND TO KEEP IT."

Mankind's first occupation began on a Rosh Hashanah. Adam's destiny is found in the earth. When he sinned, an earthquake of sorts took place. He was cast out of the realm of the Garden of Eden and cast into the realm of the Field which is also known as the word.

[GENESIS 3:23-24 KJV] "23 THEREFORE THE LORD GOD SENT HIM FORTH FROM THE GARDEN OF EDEN, TO TILL THE GROUND FROM WHENCE HE WAS TAKEN. 24 SO HE DROVE OUT THE MAN; AND HE PLACED AT THE EAST OF THE GARDEN OF EDEN CHERUBIMS, AND A FLAMING SWORD

*WHICH TURNED EVERY WAY, TO KEEP THE WAY OF
THE TREE OF LIFE."*

Adam's ministry was to cultivate and to guard
the Garden of Eden. This assignment was the
equivalent of the mission that God gave the
Israelites at the foot of Mount Sinai. The
spiritual effect of cultivating the garden was the
same as that of the 248 positive commandments
and that of the 365 negatives commandments.
There are 365 commandments in the Torah. 248
of the commandments are positive
commandments which are the "thou shalt do"
statements. The 365 negative commandments
are the "thou shalt not" statements. God taught
Adam and Eve the entire Torah in the Garden of
Eden. The Torah is the Tree of Life and it
provides advice for every aspect of life. The
Lord is also telling us to eat of the Tree of Life.
The Torah is the Tree of Life in our lives. By
learning Torah with the intention of applying it
in our daily lives, we can face every obstacle
with confidence. We don't need to learn how to
live by trial and error. We can apply Torah
concepts in our daily living. Life is not worth
living without Torah. The Torah is not some
abstract document that is only for the Sages. It
provides the blueprint for our lives. If we

approach the Torah from the perspective of the Tree of the knowledge of good and evil, then we turn Torah into a theoretical exercise with personal application. We don't study Torah in order to fill our minds with head knowledge. Rather, we study Torah in order to apply it to every aspect of our lives including education, career, child rearing, and in our relationships. God taught Adam and Eve the purpose of creation, the proper way to live, how to live, how to relate to the world, the rules for living, and societal conventions. He wants mankind to follow the Torah and thereby ascend the ladder of spiritual growth. When Adam and Eve sinned by partaking of the forbidden fruit, God exiled them into the world.

Consequently, mankind has lived in the realm of the Field ever since. Mankind has been in this exile for almost 6,000 years. Let's return to the Garden of Eden. God planted a Garden in Eden. What kind of gardening did Adam perform in the Garden? He didn't perform gardening in the sense that we understand it. Adam performed service as a priest. God commanded him to dress it and to keep. The Garden of Eden was so holy that it could not permit nor tolerate any evil. That is why Adam and Eve were exiled from the Garden after they sinned. Adam was completely engaged in service to God in the

Garden of Eden. I believe Adam failed in his service when he permitted the serpent to enter the Garden. There is a teaching here for us. Even while we are engaged in our service to God, we should be on our guard against evil. As we move forward in our service to God, we must also be on our guard to protect and guard what we have accomplished.

[REVELATION 3:2 KJV] "2 BE WATCHFUL, AND STRENGTHEN THE THINGS WHICH REMAIN, THAT ARE READY TO DIE: FOR I HAVE NOT FOUND THY WORKS PERFECT BEFORE GOD."

Where was Adam when Eve was tempted of the serpent? I don't know but it's my opinion if Adam were on guard as the protector of the Garden of Eden, then the Serpent would not have had access to tempt Eve.

[GENESIS 3:6 KJV] "6 AND WHEN THE WOMAN SAW THAT THE TREE [WAS] GOOD FOR FOOD, AND THAT IT [WAS] PLEASANT TO THE EYES, AND A TREE TO BE DESIRED TO MAKE [ONE] WISE, SHE TOOK OF THE FRUIT THEREOF, AND DID EAT, AND

GAVE ALSO UNTO HER HUSBAND WITH HER; AND
HE DID EAT."

Adam and Eve were exiled from the Garden of Eden into the world as a result of the sin of eating of the forbidden fruit. Satan was able to tempt Eve using the senses of hearing, sight, touch, and taste. There is one sense that the serpent was not able to influence and that is the sense of smell. Adam failed in his ministry of protecting the Garden of Eden.

Adam was therefore warned to guard the garden, his Divine environment, in order to ensure that his service of God be carried out with pure, ego-less love. It was, in fact, precisely in this area that Adam soon erred.

[GENESIS 8:20-22 KJV] "20 AND NOAH BUILDED AN ALTAR UNTO THE LORD; AND TOOK OF EVERY CLEAN BEAST, AND OF EVERY CLEAN FOWL, AND OFFERED BURNT OFFERINGS ON THE ALTAR. 21 AND THE LORD SMELLED A SWEET SAVOUR; AND THE LORD SAID IN HIS HEART, I WILL NOT AGAIN CURSE THE GROUND ANY MORE FOR MAN'S SAKE; FOR THE IMAGINATION OF

*MAN'S HEART [IS] EVIL FROM HIS YOUTH;
NEITHER WILL I AGAIN SMITE ANY MORE EVERY
THING LIVING, AS I HAVE DONE. 22 WHILE THE
EARTH REMAINETH, SEEDTIME AND HARVEST, AND
COLD AND HEAT, AND SUMMER AND WINTER, AND
DAY AND NIGHT SHALL NOT CEASE."*

THE FEAST OF TABERNACLES

[LEVITICUS 23:34 KJV] "34 SPEAK UNTO THE CHILDREN OF ISRAEL, SAYING, THE FIFTEENTH DAY OF THIS SEVENTH MONTH [SHALL BE] THE FEAST OF TABERNACLES [FOR] SEVEN DAYS UNTO THE LORD."

The Feast of Tabernacles is also known as Sukkot. Sukkot is celebrated for seven days from the 15th to the 21st day of the 7th month, the month of Tishrei. The 7th and final day of Sukkot is known as Hoshana Rabba. The Book of Life and its verdict is delivered. We begin the new year with a clean slate. On Rosh Hashanah, we accepted the sovereignty of God over our lives. All of creation passed before the Judgment Seat of God. Our names are written in the Book of Life. Ten days later, on Yom Kippur, the Day of Atonement, our destinies are sealed for the coming year. Sukkot comes five days after Yom Kippur. Once we have reached a new level of purity and atonement on Yom Kippur, we can then experience the joy of Sukkot. On Sukkot, our hearts experience the true joy of the redemption of the entire world. Sukkot commemorates how protective "Clouds of Glory" surrounded the Israelites after leaving Egypt during the forty years of their sojourn in the desert. It also commemorates how the Israelites lived in temporary dwellings during that same time. So too we leave the safety and security of our houses and put ourselves under the direct protection of the Lord. His protection is what really matters. Numbers 10:34 tells us that the Cloud was on them by day as they pulled up stakes from the camp.

In connection with the journeys of Israel, the Torah mentions the cloud seven times to allude to seven separate clouds that accompanied them. Four of the clouds protected the Israelite camp in four directions: north, south, east, and west. One cloud hovered above Israel. One cloud cushioned their feet from the elements of the ground including the hot and rocky desert floor. The seventh cloud went ahead of the Israelites to ease their way either by leveling the mountains or by filling in the recessions of the valleys. (Rashi).

During Sukkot, the Israelites would dwell in booths or tents for seven days in order to commemorate their journey in the Wilderness.

[LEVITICUS 23:41-42 KJV] "41 AND YE SHALL KEEP IT A FEAST UNTO THE LORD SEVEN DAYS IN THE YEAR. [IT SHALL BE] A STATUTE FOR EVER IN YOUR GENERATIONS: YE SHALL CELEBRATE IT IN THE SEVENTH MONTH. 42 YE SHALL DWELL IN BOOTHS SEVEN DAYS; ALL THAT ARE ISRAELITES BORN SHALL DWELL IN BOOTHS:"

Sukkot is the only festival that our prayer is described as a time of our joy. This is because Sukkot is a time of culmination, a time when the individual and the nation have succeeded in attaining a long-sought goal. Spiritually, Sukkot is the culmination of a process. First comes redemption during Pesach, then the purpose of redemption at the receiving of the Torah during Shavuot, and finally, these lessons are brought into our everyday lives when we find our joy in observing the commandments during Sukkot. In addition, Sukkot is the culmination of the Tishrei process of repentance and atonement, when we succeed in dragging ourselves out of the morass of sin. Assembling in tents speaks of dedicating ourselves to the service of God, the study of His word, and a sojourn in His Sanctuary before returning to everyday life.

The 7th day of Sukkot (Tishrei 21) is known as the day of "Great Salvation." It is a day of praise to the Lord.

The culmination of creation will occur when we enter into our ministries as kings and priests to God. The purpose of creation is to bring the knowledge of God into the world.

[HABAKKUK 2:14 KJV] "14 FOR THE EARTH SHALL BE FILLED WITH THE KNOWLEDGE OF THE GLORY OF THE LORD, AS THE WATERS COVER THE SEA."

This is why God created the Heavens and the Earth. It was God's desire to fill the earth with the knowledge of His glory. The Feast of Tabernacles is the culmination of God's plan. We also see the culmination of this process in the Book of Revelation:

[REVELATION 21:2-4 KJV] "2 AND I JOHN SAW THE HOLY CITY, NEW JERUSALEM, COMING DOWN FROM GOD OUT OF HEAVEN, PREPARED AS A BRIDE ADORNED FOR HER HUSBAND. 3 AND I HEARD A GREAT VOICE OUT OF HEAVEN SAYING,

BEHOLD, THE TABERNACLE OF GOD [IS] WITH MEN, AND HE WILL DWELL WITH THEM, AND THEY SHALL BE HIS PEOPLE, AND GOD HIMSELF SHALL BE WITH THEM, [AND BE] THEIR GOD. 4 AND GOD SHALL WIPE AWAY ALL TEARS FROM THEIR EYES; AND THERE SHALL BE NO MORE DEATH, NEITHER SORROW, NOR CRYING, NEITHER SHALL THERE BE ANY MORE PAIN: FOR THE FORMER THINGS ARE PASSED AWAY."

Imagine a day when every tear is wiped away. This will take place when Messiah comes.

SOLOMON'S WISDOM

Solomon's wisdom was connected with the earth. Solomon was only 12 years old when he succeeded his father, King David. He attempted to infiltrate the world with holiness and elevate it to holiness. He married countless foreign wives in order to build peaceful relationships with the nations of the earth. The first request that King Solomon made of the Lord was wisdom:

[1 KINGS 3:5-6 KJV] "5 IN GIBEON THE LORD APPEARED TO SOLOMON IN A DREAM BY NIGHT: AND GOD SAID, ASK WHAT I SHALL GIVE THEE. 6 AND SOLOMON SAID, THOU HAST SHEWED UNTO THY SERVANT DAVID MY FATHER GREAT MERCY, ACCORDING AS HE WALKED BEFORE THEE IN TRUTH, AND IN RIGHTEOUSNESS, AND IN UPRIGHTNESS OF HEART WITH THEE; AND THOU HAST KEPT FOR HIM THIS GREAT KINDNESS, THAT THOU HAST GIVEN HIM A SON TO SIT ON HIS THRONE, AS [IT IS] THIS DAY."

In an unprecedented demonstration of favor, God appeared to Solomon and offered to give him whatever he desired. This is how Solomon responded:

1 KINGS 3:8-9 KJV] "8 AND THY SERVANT [IS] IN THE MIDST OF THY PEOPLE WHICH THOU HAST CHOSEN, A GREAT PEOPLE, THAT CANNOT BE NUMBERED NOR COUNTED FOR MULTITUDE. 9 GIVE THEREFORE THY SERVANT AN UNDERSTANDING HEART TO JUDGE THY PEOPLE, THAT I MAY DISCERN BETWEEN GOOD AND BAD:

FOR WHO IS ABLE TO JUDGE THIS THY SO GREAT A PEOPLE?"

Would you have made the same request if the Lord offered you anything you wanted? This request so pleased the Lord:

[1 KINGS 3:10-11 KJV] "10 AND THE SPEECH PLEASED THE LORD, THAT SOLOMON HAD ASKED THIS THING. 11 AND GOD SAID UNTO HIM, BECAUSE THOU HAST ASKED THIS THING, AND HAST NOT ASKED FOR THYSELF LONG LIFE; NEITHER HAST ASKED RICHES FOR THYSELF, NOR HAST ASKED THE LIFE OF THINE ENEMIES; BUT HAST ASKED FOR THYSELF UNDERSTANDING TO DISCERN JUDGMENT; "

Let's remove the "Disney" from the story. This is not like Aladdin rubbing an oil lamp 3 times. Next, a genie comes out of the bottle and offers him 3 wishes in payment for granting him freedom. This is often how we read the Biblical text and thus we turn our Lord into a wish granter. We should not cheapen the Lord into a wish granter. The Lord was actually testing King Solomon to see what request he would make. The Lord will also do the same thing in our lives. He will offer us opportunities to request whatever we want to see if we are focused on the Kingdom of Heaven or on material things. Let's make the same request as Solomon by focusing on the Kingdom of Heaven in our requests. Even as a 12-year old, Solomon demonstrated maturity, by requesting only wisdom and understanding in order to execute justice for God's people. Only a righteous, God-fearing person would make such a request. Solomon wished to serve God without a desire for any reward. When you serve God without desire for any reward but just a sincere desire to please Him, God will multiply your reward. Perkie Avos says:

[AVOS 1:3] "3 BE NOT LIKE A SERVANT WHO SERVES HIS MASTER IN ORDER TO RECEIVE REWARD"

As a result of the Lord granting Solomon his request, Solomon received such mastery of the Torah that virtually nothing was hidden from him. The Sages says that he was even able to decipher the communications of birds and animals. If you read through Song of Songs,

Proverbs, and Ecclesiastes, then you will see the wisdom of Solomon that was connected to the earth. Consider the following examples in the Solomon's books:

[PROVERBS 6:6 KJV] "6 GO TO THE ANT, THOU SLUGGARD; CONSIDER HER WAYS, AND BE WISE:"

[ECCLESIASTES 1:7 KJV] "7 ALL THE RIVERS RUN INTO THE SEA; YET THE SEA [IS] NOT FULL; UNTO THE PLACE FROM WHENCE THE RIVERS COME, THITHER THEY RETURN AGAIN."

[SONG OF SONGS 1:17 KJV] "17 THE BEAMS OF OUR HOUSE [ARE] CEDAR, [AND] OUR RAFTERS OF FIR."

Solomon used things that were of the earth to explain heavenly concepts. Solomon used an approach that I call the bottom-up approach in his ministry. Solomon wanted to elevate everything from the ground-up including the building of the Temple. He sought to bring more awareness of God into the world. Solomon possessed the ability to present the Torah in such a magnificent way using proverbs and parables that people could understand at their own level. A genius cannot typically relate intelligence to a person of average intelligence. Solomon, in contrast was able to teach everyone regardless of their Torah IQ. He spoke of the trees. According to my research, Solomon instructed people about the scientific and medical properties of each species of flora and fauna. He understood the underlying reasons for the Torah's laws regarding all creatures. His wisdom was even superior to that of the angels. He understood the workings of animals and plants. Dignitaries from all over the world came to hear him speak:

[1 KINGS 4:34 KJV] "34 AND THERE CAME OF ALL PEOPLE TO HEAR THE WISDOM OF SOLOMON, FROM ALL KINGS OF THE EARTH, WHICH HAD HEARD OF HIS WISDOM."

Through his wisdom, he was able to build peaceful relations with the nations and acquire materials for the building of a magnificent Temple for God's glory. Solomon's Temple was the most magnificent of all constructions in the world.

[1 KINGS 10:21 KJV] "21 AND ALL KING SOLOMON'S DRINKING VESSELS [WERE OF] GOLD, AND ALL THE VESSELS OF THE HOUSE OF THE FOREST OF LEBANON [WERE OF] PURE GOLD; NONE [WERE OF] SILVER: IT WAS NOTHING ACCOUNTED OF IN THE DAYS OF SOLOMON."

Gold was so abundant in Solomon's court that even the cups were made of gold. There was no silver because silver had no value in Solomon's days. There was no longing for money because people longed for the wisdom of King Solomon. Silver was literally worthless in their eyes. This was the bottom-up approach that Solomon used. In contrast, Solomon's father, King David, used the top-down approach in his ministry. Instead, he sought to infuse the world with holiness by drawing down God's glory from heaven to earth. David was always connected with Heaven and sought to draw down holiness into the earth.

CHAPTER 3 - WIND

THE SPIRIT OF GOD

[JOHN 3:8 KJV] "8 THE WIND BLOWETH WHERE IT LISTETH, AND THOU HEAREST THE SOUND THEREOF, BUT CANST NOT TELL WHENCE IT COMETH, AND WHITHER IT GOETH: SO IS EVERY ONE THAT IS BORN OF THE SPIRIT."

The wind is often used as a representation of the moving of the Spirit of God. Jesus said this about one who is born of the Spirit: "canst not tell whence it cometh, and whiter it goeth." When you give the Spirit of God permission to take over your life, it is He who takes over. Our life is a journey in the Spirit.

[MATTHEW 4:1 KJV] "1 THEN WAS JESUS LED UP OF THE SPIRIT INTO THE WILDERNESS TO BE TEMPTED OF THE DEVIL."

After Jesus' baptism by John, Jesus was driven into the wilderness. Being driven is a representation of being carried by the Spirit. Often the Spirit of God will take you where you don't want to go. I can think of no better example than Jonah.

YONAH (JONAH), MERCY, REPENTANCE, AND YOM KIPPUR

[JONAH 1:1 KJV] "1 NOW THE WORD OF THE LORD CAME UNTO JONAH THE SON OF AMITTAI, SAYING,"

Jonah received the call from God. This is a word that Jonah didn't want to receive. In order to dispel any preconceptions that you may have about Jonah, I would like to tell you that Jonah is one of my favorite people in the Bible. The story of Jonah truly shows the working of the Spirit of God like the wind in our lives. Before we continue this fascinating study about the call of God on Jonah's life, let's talk about Jonah's origins.

[1 KINGS 17:8-9, 13 KJV] "8 AND THE WORD OF THE LORD CAME UNTO HIM, SAYING, 9 ARISE, GET THEE TO ZAREPHATH, WHICH BELONGETH TO ZIDON, AND DWELL THERE: BEHOLD, I HAVE COMMANDED A WIDOW WOMAN THERE TO SUSTAIN THEE. ... 13 AND ELIJAH SAID UNTO HER, FEAR NOT; GO [AND] DO AS THOU HAST SAID: BUT MAKE ME THEREOF A LITTLE CAKE FIRST, AND BRING [IT] UNTO ME, AND AFTER MAKE FOR THEE AND FOR THY SON.

The Lord sent Elijah to the widow of Zarephath. We often use this scripture to describe how the Lord sustains us even in the midst of calamity. Have you ever asked who her son was. This son was the prophet, Jonah. The widow of Zarephath had been the wife of the prophet, Amitai. Jonah was one of the greatest prophets of his time.

[1 KINGS 17:17-23 KJV] 17 AND IT CAME TO PASS AFTER THESE THINGS, [THAT] THE SON OF THE WOMAN, THE MISTRESS OF THE HOUSE, FELL

SICK; AND HIS SICKNESS WAS SO SORE, THAT
THERE WAS NO BREATH LEFT IN HIM. 18 AND SHE
SAID UNTO ELIJAH, WHAT HAVE I TO DO WITH
THEE, O THOU MAN OF GOD? ART THOU COME
UNTO ME TO CALL MY SIN TO REMEMBRANCE, AND
TO SLAY MY SON? 19 AND HE SAID UNTO HER,
GIVE ME THY SON. AND HE TOOK HIM OUT OF
HER BOSOM, AND CARRIED HIM UP INTO A LOFT,
WHERE HE ABODE, AND LAID HIM UPON HIS OWN
BED. 20 AND HE CRIED UNTO THE LORD, AND
SAID, O LORD MY GOD, HAST THOU ALSO
BROUGHT EVIL UPON THE WIDOW WITH WHOM I
SOJOURN, BY SLAYING HER SON? 21 AND HE
STRETCHED HIMSELF UPON THE CHILD THREE
TIMES, AND CRIED UNTO THE LORD, AND SAID, O
LORD MY GOD, I PRAY THEE, LET THIS CHILD'S
SOUL COME INTO HIM AGAIN. 22 AND THE LORD
HEARD THE VOICE OF ELIJAH; AND THE SOUL OF
THE CHILD CAME INTO HIM AGAIN, AND HE
REVIVED. 23 AND ELIJAH TOOK THE CHILD, AND
BROUGHT HIM DOWN OUT OF THE CHAMBER INTO
THE HOUSE, AND DELIVERED HIM UNTO HIS
MOTHER: AND ELIJAH SAID, SEE, THY SON
LIVETH. 24 AND THE WOMAN SAID TO ELIJAH,
NOW BY THIS I KNOW THAT THOU [ART] A MAN OF

This same child, Jonah was brought back to life by Elijah. Not only was Elisha part of Elijah's mission, Jonah was also part of his mission. God not only used Elijah to bring back the child, Jonah to life, He also used Elijah to raise up a great prophet. After this tremendous miracle, the widow of Zarephath prophesied: "Now by this I know that thou [art] a man of God, [and] that the word of the LORD in thy mouth [is] truth." Elijah possessed a mantle or anointing of truth. Jonah was called the son of Amittai. Amittai means truth. Jonah was called the son of truth. Jonah was a completely righteous man.

The prophet Elijah was dispatched to Zarephath where he was told a widow would provide for him. Jonah's life was part of Elijah's mission. Jonah became the living demonstration of the power of God, through His prophet. He was ben Amittai, the son of truth, man of truth. The young Jonah became Elijah's disciple and, when Elijah ascended to heaven, Jonah became the disciple of Elisha. The reason why I love Jonah so much is because he defended the honor of Israel so much. I will explain this in detail shortly. Please stay with me.

THE CALL TO NINEVEH

[JONAH 1:2 KJV] "2 ARISE, GO TO NINEVEH, THAT GREAT CITY, AND CRY AGAINST IT; FOR THEIR WICKEDNESS IS COME UP BEFORE ME."

Nineveh was a tremendous city that was part of the Assyrian empire, an empire that would eventually take the 10 northern tribes of Israel into captivity. Nineveh was infamous for its wickedness and it was an enemy of Israel. The sins of Nineveh were especially offensive to God in the areas of robbery and oppression. These sins parallel the sins of the Generation of the Flood and the sins of Sodom:

[GENESIS 6:11 KJV] "11 THE EARTH ALSO WAS CORRUPT BEFORE GOD, AND THE EARTH WAS FILLED WITH VIOLENCE."

[GENESIS 13:13 KJV] "13 BUT THE MEN OF SODOM [WERE] WICKED AND SINNERS BEFORE THE LORD EXCEEDINGLY."

Jonah proclaimed Nineveh's impending destruction within 40 days. What is the significance of 40 days? Again, I must take you back to the Biblical feasts to explain the secret of the 40 days. There are 40 days between the first day of the 6th month to the 10th day of the 7th month on the Hebrew calendar. The 6th month is called Elul. The seventh month is called Tishrei. We know that the first day of the Tishrei is Rosh Hashanah. The 10th day of the 7th month is known as Yom Kippur, the Day of Atonement. Yom Kippur is the holiest day of the entire year. The 40 days from Elul to Yom Kippur have been designated by Heaven as a time when repentance (teshuvah) is most accessible. Most of take repentance for granted. What came first, sin or repentance? Before you continue reading, please take a moment to ponder this question. It's almost like asking the question, "What came first: the chicken or the egg?" Our natural response is to say that sin preceded repentance. In terms of our actions, that is true. The Sages teach us that repentance was created even before the universe was created. Imagine if God created us without access to teshuvah. Under those rules, God would have had to destroy His creation after Adam and Eve sinned. Thank God for the gift of teshuvah.

Our destinies for the coming year, in all aspects of life, are determined on Rosh Hashanah and sealed on Yom Kippur. I am actually writing this section of the book on Rosh Hashanah. We should apply our efforts to perform sincere acts of teshuvah. This should be our destiny driven mission. In fact, I am asking the Lord to bring to remembrance sins that I have not repented of yet. These 40 days have been designated as "eis ratzon," an extraordinary time of favor that is charged with Divine compassion.

[ISAIAH 55:6 KJV] "6 SEEK YE THE LORD WHILE HE MAY BE FOUND, CALL YE UPON HIM WHILE HE IS NEAR:"

JONAH FLEES FROM THE PRESENCE OF THE LORD

[JONAH 1:3 KJV] "3 BUT JONAH ROSE UP TO FLEE UNTO TARSHISH FROM THE PRESENCE OF THE LORD, AND WENT DOWN TO JOPPA; AND HE FOUND A SHIP GOING TO TARSHISH: SO HE PAID THE FARE THEREOF, AND WENT DOWN INTO IT, TO

GO WITH THEM UNTO TARSHISH FROM THE PRESENCE OF THE LORD. "

At the children's Sunday School level reading of the text, the story seems so simple. It is much more complex than what meets the eye. The Lord's unfathomable mercy comes to mind as I read this text. Per Artscroll Jonah, "The story of Jonah is deceptively simple. Upon careful analysis, it presents mind-boggling difficulties." Why does Jonah flee from his mission? We typically read the story as follows:

- The Lord commissions Jonah to preach repentance to a sinful city lest it be destroyed.

- Jonah flees from the Lord's Presence and boards a cruise ship for Tashish.

- The cruise ship is hit by a horrible storm.

- The prophet is thrown overboard to save the ship's crew and passengers from destruction.

- Jonah is swallowed up by a whale.

- Jonah spends 3 days in the belly of a whale.

- Jonah is spewed onto the shore of Nineveh.

- Jonah preaches repentance to the Ninevites and the city's inhabitants repent and are saved from destruction.

- Jonah is now upset because they repented. He felt that God's mercy was unjustified.

JONAH'S ANGUISH

[JONAH 4:1-3 KJV] "1 BUT IT DISPLEASED JONAH EXCEEDINGLY, AND HE WAS VERY ANGRY. 2 AND HE PRAYED UNTO THE LORD, AND SAID, I PRAY THEE, O LORD, [WAS] NOT THIS MY SAYING, WHEN I WAS YET IN MY COUNTRY? THEREFORE I FLED BEFORE UNTO TARSHISH: FOR I KNEW THAT THOU [ART] A GRACIOUS GOD, AND MERCIFUL, SLOW TO ANGER, AND OF GREAT KINDNESS, AND REPENTEST THEE OF THE EVIL. 3 THEREFORE NOW, O LORD, TAKE, I BESEECH THEE, MY LIFE FROM ME; FOR [IT IS] BETTER FOR ME TO DIE THAN TO LIVE."

Jonah's story bears the message of a repentance that only God could comprehend. At the surface level reading of the text, Jonah appears to be just an angry old rebellious prophet. I always wondered why the book of Jonah was in the Bible. It wasn't until I read the Artscroll's Yonah / Jonah by Rabbi Meir Zlotowitz[iii] that I began to understand Jonah. As a result of my study, Jonah has become one of my favorite prophets in the Tanakh. The question I struggled with was how could Jonah refuse to obey the command of God? Being a man of God, he must have known that he could not run from the Presence of the Lord. You can't just put God on mute. How could he attempt to flee from prophecy? Why was he against preaching repentance to the Ninevites? How could God use such an angry man in a tremendous way? Was he prejudiced against the people? Why was he so angry when a massive revival of repentance took place? You would think this was the highlight and the greatest accomplishment of Jonah's ministry. In fact, the repentance demonstrated by the people of Ninevah has become the benchmark of repentance throughout history. Even Jesus used Ninevah in his rebuke against His generation:

[LUKE 11:30 KJV] "30 FOR AS JONAS WAS A SIGN UNTO THE NINEVITES, SO SHALL ALSO THE SON OF MAN BE TO THIS GENERATION."

Now let's dive into Jonah's dilemma. Jonah knowing that the Israelites of the Northern Kingdom of Israel would not repent of their wickedness was angry when the Ninevites repented of their wickedness. Moreover, Jonah knew that the Assyrians would conquer the Northern Kingdom of Israel in the future. Ninevah was the capital of the Assyrian empire. Jonah was being sent by God to preach repentance to the future conquerors of Israel. Jonah saw himself as being used to facilitate the future exile of the Northern Kingdom. Can you see Jonah's dilemma? Jonah so loved his people that he was willing to risk his own life for the sake of Israel. This is why the Lord so honored Jonah. One of the keys to become a successful leader is to put others above yourself. This is exactly what Jonah demonstrated. Jonah did not comprehend God's attribute of mercy. How can anyone of us comprehend God's mercy towards those that demonstrate such wickedness. I cannot begin to fathom God's mercy towards the Nazis during the Holocaust. This is something I may never understand. God's ways are much higher than my ways:

[ISAIAH 55:9 KJV] "9 FOR [AS] THE HEAVENS ARE HIGHER THAN THE EARTH, SO ARE MY WAYS HIGHER THAN YOUR WAYS, AND MY THOUGHTS THAN YOUR THOUGHTS."

Even though I cannot comprehend God's Mercy, I choose to trust in His Mercy and Divine Providence. God governs the world by the 13 attributes of Mercy. I will share the 13 attributes of God's Mercy later in this book.

God's Providence is one of the themes in the Book of Jonah. Divine Providence extends to the entire earth. God's Mercy is accessible to the entire world. No one can run away from God's Presence. David said:

[PSALM 139:7-8 KJV] "7 WHITHER SHALL I GO FROM THY SPIRIT? OR WHITHER SHALL I FLEE FROM THY PRESENCE? 8 IF I ASCEND UP INTO HEAVEN, THOU [ART] THERE: IF I MAKE MY BED IN HELL, BEHOLD, THOU [ART THERE]."

God's mercy is boundless. His gift of repentance enables us to return to Him. The

Rabbis tell us that seven things were created before the world:

1. The Torah, for it is written:

   [PROVERBS 8:22 KJV] "22 THE LORD POSSESSED ME IN THE BEGINNING OF HIS WAY, BEFORE HIS WORKS OF OLD."

2. Repentance, for it is written:

   [PSALM 90:2-3 KJV] "2 BEFORE THE MOUNTAINS WERE BROUGHT FORTH, OR EVER THOU HADST FORMED THE EARTH AND THE WORLD, EVEN FROM EVERLASTING TO EVERLASTING, THOU [ART] GOD. 3 THOU TURNEST MAN TO DESTRUCTION; AND SAYEST, RETURN, YE CHILDREN OF MEN."

3. The Garden of Eden, for it is written:

   [GENESIS 2:8 KJV] "8 AND THE LORD GOD PLANTED A GARDEN EASTWARD IN EDEN; AND THERE HE PUT THE MAN WHOM HE HAD FORMED."

   The Garden of Eden was planted from

aforetime.

4. Gehenna

5. The Throne of Glory, for it is written:

   [PSALM 93:2 KJV] "2 THY THRONE [IS] ESTABLISHED OF OLD: THOU [ART] FROM EVERLASTING."

6. The Temple, for it is written,

   [PSALM 93:2 KJV] "2 THY THRONE [IS] ESTABLISHED OF OLD: THOU [ART] FROM EVERLASTING."

7. The Name of the Messiah, for it is written:

   [PSALM 72:17 KJV] "17 HIS NAME SHALL ENDURE FOR EVER: HIS NAME SHALL BE CONTINUED AS LONG AS THE SUN: AND [MEN] SHALL BE BLESSED IN HIM: ALL NATIONS SHALL CALL HIM BLESSED."

The second thing created before the creation was Repentance. If God created us without the gift of repentance, then mankind would have become extinct after Adam and Eve committed the sin of eating the forbidden fruit:

[GENESIS 3:11 KJV] "11 AND HE SAID, WHO TOLD THEE THAT THOU [WAST] NAKED? HAST THOU EATEN OF THE TREE, WHEREOF I COMMANDED THEE THAT THOU SHOULDEST NOT EAT?"

God created Adam and Eve with the Name, Elohim Adonai which is the Name that denotes God's Mercy:

[GENESIS 1:27 KJV] "27 SO GOD CREATED MAN IN HIS [OWN] IMAGE, IN THE IMAGE OF GOD CREATED HE HIM; MALE AND FEMALE CREATED HE THEM."

The gift of repentance gives us the grace to return and rise after we have fallen. Often after repentance, we can arise to a greater stature than we had before we sinned. One of the greatest acts of repentance recorded in the Tanakh was David's act of repentance after he was confronted by the prophet Nathan for sinning with Bathsheba:

[2 SAMUEL 12:7-13 KJV] "7 AND NATHAN SAID TO DAVID, THOU [ART] THE MAN. THUS SAITH THE LORD GOD OF ISRAEL, I ANOINTED THEE KING OVER ISRAEL, AND I DELIVERED THEE OUT OF THE HAND OF SAUL; 8 AND I GAVE THEE THY MASTER'S HOUSE, AND THY MASTER'S WIVES INTO THY BOSOM, AND GAVE THEE THE HOUSE OF ISRAEL AND OF JUDAH; AND IF [THAT HAD BEEN] TOO LITTLE, I WOULD MOREOVER HAVE GIVEN UNTO THEE SUCH AND SUCH THINGS. 9 WHEREFORE HAST THOU DESPISED THE COMMANDMENT OF THE LORD, TO DO EVIL IN HIS SIGHT? THOU HAST KILLED URIAH THE HITTITE WITH THE SWORD, AND HAST TAKEN HIS WIFE [TO BE] THY WIFE, AND HAST SLAIN HIM WITH THE SWORD OF THE CHILDREN OF AMMON. 10 NOW THEREFORE THE SWORD SHALL NEVER DEPART FROM THINE HOUSE; BECAUSE THOU HAST DESPISED ME, AND HAST TAKEN THE WIFE

*OF URIAH THE HITTITE TO BE THY WIFE. 11 THUS
SAITH THE LORD, BEHOLD, I WILL RAISE UP EVIL
AGAINST THEE OUT OF THINE OWN HOUSE, AND I
WILL TAKE THY WIVES BEFORE THINE EYES, AND
GIVE [THEM] UNTO THY NEIGHBOUR, AND HE
SHALL LIE WITH THY WIVES IN THE SIGHT OF THIS
SUN. 12 FOR THOU DIDST [IT] SECRETLY: BUT I
WILL DO THIS THING BEFORE ALL ISRAEL, AND
BEFORE THE SUN. 13 AND DAVID SAID UNTO
NATHAN, I HAVE SINNED AGAINST THE LORD.
AND NATHAN SAID UNTO DAVID, THE LORD
ALSO HATH PUT AWAY THY SIN; THOU SHALT NOT
DIE. "*

After David's repentance, he left home to lead a successful military campaign against Ammon.

*[2 SAMUEL 12:29 KJV] "29 AND DAVID
GATHERED ALL THE PEOPLE TOGETHER, AND
WENT TO RABBAH, AND FOUGHT AGAINST IT, AND
TOOK IT. "*

Sometimes a sin improves a man more than a number of good deeds. David was already great but now he became greater. Taking ownership for our shortcoming and performing acts of repentance can cause us to become greater. That is the paradox of sin such that repentance enables one to rise to greater heights than that which was possible before the sin. When we sin, we are confronted with the knowledge that our relationship with the Lord may not be strong enough to keep us from sinning. We must then work on establishing a connection with God in that area that will help us get victory in that area. Any area of our lives that are void of God's presence can be an open door for sin to enter in. If we struggle with impure thoughts, then we need to fill our minds with Torah.

Does the desire of achieving greater heights give us the license to sin? Certainly not! We should not abuse the gift given to us as Paul tells us:

[ROMANS 6:1-4 KJV] "1 WHAT SHALL WE SAY THEN? SHALL WE CONTINUE IN SIN, THAT GRACE MAY ABOUND? 2 GOD FORBID. HOW SHALL WE, THAT ARE DEAD TO SIN, LIVE ANY LONGER THEREIN? 3 KNOW YE NOT, THAT SO MANY OF US AS WERE BAPTIZED INTO JESUS CHRIST WERE BAPTIZED INTO HIS DEATH? 4 THEREFORE WE

ARE BURIED WITH HIM BY BAPTISM INTO DEATH: THAT LIKE AS CHRIST WAS RAISED UP FROM THE DEAD BY THE GLORY OF THE FATHER, EVEN SO WE ALSO SHOULD WALK IN NEWNESS OF LIFE."

Now let's get back to the creation of the heavens and the earth. The heavens and the earth were created with the Name, Elohim which is the Name that denotes God's strict justice:

[GENESIS 1:1 KJV] "1 IN THE BEGINNING GOD CREATED THE HEAVEN AND THE EARTH."

The heavens and the earth don't have free will. They don't have the option to disobey God. Because of the gift of free-will bestowed upon us by God, we need the gift of repentance to help us arise when we sin.

In summary, the wind represents one being sent where he or she don't want to go. For example, Jesus was driven into the wilderness by the Spirit of God after His baptism:

[MATTHEW 4:1 KJV] "1 THEN WAS JESUS LED UP OF THE SPIRIT INTO THE WILDERNESS TO BE TEMPTED OF THE DEVIL."

The Lord sent a great wind into the sea to cause Jonah to repent:

[JONAH 1:4 KJV] "4 BUT THE LORD SENT OUT A GREAT WIND INTO THE SEA, AND THERE WAS A MIGHTY TEMPEST IN THE SEA, SO THAT THE SHIP WAS LIKE TO BE BROKEN."

CHAPTER 4 - FIRE

A COVENANT OF FIRE

[GENESIS 1:1 KJV] "1 IN THE BEGINNING GOD CREATED THE HEAVEN AND THE EARTH."

According to <u>The Call Of The Torah: 5 – Devarim</u>, the letters of the words "In the beginning" from Genesis 1:1 can be rearranged in Hebrew to read, "a covenant of fire." [iv] In Hebrew, letters in words can be rearranged to reveal prophetic messages. The Sages have discovered prophetic interpretations of Biblical texts throughout the ages using this method. A "Covenant of Fire" is a reference to the burning bush that Moses saw while tending his sheep upon the mountain of God:

[EXODUS 3:2 KJV] "2 AND THE ANGEL OF THE LORD APPEARED UNTO HIM IN A FLAME OF FIRE OUT OF THE MIDST OF A BUSH: AND HE LOOKED,

AND, BEHOLD, THE BUSH BURNED WITH FIRE, AND THE BUSH [WAS] NOT CONSUMED."

Even as God gave His covenant with Israel in the midst of thunder and lightning on Mount Sinai after the exodus from Egypt, God made Himself known to Moses in the burning bush in order to demonstrate His love for Israel prior to the exodus. Let's enter into the fire.

THE FIERY AFFLICTION

[EXODUS 2:11 KJV] "11 AND IT CAME TO PASS IN THOSE DAYS, WHEN MOSES WAS GROWN, THAT HE WENT OUT UNTO HIS BRETHREN, AND LOOKED ON THEIR BURDENS: AND HE SPIED AN EGYPTIAN SMITING AN HEBREW, ONE OF HIS BRETHREN."

In order to comprehend the fire, you must be in touch with people's suffering. The Torah is not telling us that Moses is grown up just to tell us he is an adult. The Torah is telling us that Moses had matured to full stature both spiritually and emotionally. To be fully grown, had to be completely in touch with the sufferings of God's people. Sometimes we detach ourselves from the pain and suffering of others. If you want to be used by God, then I encourage you to connect with the sufferings of others. I believe God was testing Moses to see if he was ready to be used by Him to lead the Israelites. God didn't need proof to determine if Moses was ready for the job. God knows everything. God was testing Moses to help him know he was ready. God will not place any test before you that you are not ready for. In God's university, there are many opportunities to retake the exams that you fail. In Exodus 2:11, did you notice that he spied an Egyptian smiting an Hebrew? I never gave this much thought before but in order to spy someone you really have to be engaged with the situation. Moses really took the time to identify with his people. He even learned what was going on in secret. As a leader, you cannot turn a blind eye to the truth. Moses passed the test with flying colors. He identified with the burdens of the people and he became God's instrument to lead God's people. This is the first step in order to identify with the fire of God. Also, it was not known that Moses was a Hebrew because he was raised in Pharaoh's palace as a prince. He didn't turn a blind eye to the mistreatment of the Hebrews and when he saw a Hebrew man being mistreated by an Egyptian, he defended the Hebrew man.

[EXODUS 3:2-4 KJV] "2 AND THE ANGEL OF THE LORD APPEARED UNTO HIM IN A FLAME OF FIRE OUT OF THE MIDST OF A BUSH: AND HE LOOKED, AND, BEHOLD, THE BUSH BURNED WITH FIRE, AND THE BUSH [WAS] NOT CONSUMED. 3 AND MOSES SAID, I WILL NOW TURN ASIDE, AND SEE THIS GREAT SIGHT, WHY THE BUSH IS NOT BURNT. 4 AND WHEN THE LORD SAW THAT HE TURNED

ASIDE TO SEE, GOD CALLED UNTO HIM OUT OF THE MIDST OF THE BUSH, AND SAID, MOSES, MOSES. AND HE SAID, HERE [AM] I."

The fire of God is often connected with one feeling the burdens of others. In the Book of Exodus, Moses looked upon the burdens of the Israelites. The Midrash Rabbah says that at the time of this incident, Moses was pondering the Jewish people's situation in cruel bondage and enslavement under the Egyptians and that the Egyptians might consume Israel. While he was pondering the Israelites' predicament, God showed him a fire that burned in a thorn bush that did not consume the thorn bush. God revealed to Moses that just as the fire could not consume the thorn bush, likewise the Egyptians will not be able to consume the Israelites. The thorn bush represented Israel. Moses had just experienced his first prophetic vision with countless more to follow. The symbol of the burning bush represented Israel in Egyptian exile. This experience was a test from heaven. Where was Moses when he received this vision? He was tending his father-in-law, Jethro's flock on Mount Sinai. This is the same place that God was going to bring the Israelites in the future to receive the 10 Commandments. This is the place where Heaven came down to Earth. Now I will explain the test. Moses turned to see the sight of

the glorious vision. Moses could have ignored
the burdens of his people and enjoyed his new
life as a shepherd of Jethro's flock. I think he
was a bit overqualified for the position.
Actually, he was way overqualified. Prior to
escaping from Egypt, Moses was a prince in
Pharaoh's palace. God was preparing Moses to
become the first leader of a nation and the
greatest Torah scholar of all generations. When
Moses turned to see the sight of the bush that
was not consumed by the fire, it demonstrated
that Moses turned to see the burdens of the
Israelites. Moses passed the test by connecting
with the burdens of his people. As soon as he
passed this test, God spoke to him out of the
fiery bush. The Lord will also speak to you in
the midst of fire. What fires are you
experiencing in your life? What burden is the
Lord calling you to identify with? He turned to
see the burdens of the Israelites. When God saw
that he was connected with the afflictions of the
people, God called out to him. According to
Midrash Tachuma, God called out to Moses in
the voice of his father, Amram. God did this as
to not startle him. God will also call out to you
in a voice that you are familiar with. Before God
will speak to you, He may require that you look
at the burdens of others with empathy. Seeing
and identifying with the burdens of others is
seeing God in the fire. Again, according to
Midrash Tanchuma, Moses rejoiced saying his
father still lives. God then responded, "I am not

your father, but the God of your father."

[EXODUS 3:5 KJV] "5 AND HE SAID, DRAW NOT NIGH HITHER: PUT OFF THY SHOES FROM OFF THY FEET, FOR THE PLACE WHEREON THOU STANDEST [IS] HOLY GROUND."

Removing your shoes represents that Moses was to give himself up without reservations - without any impediment between himself and the holy ground. You too must respond without impediment to the call of God. Remember the example of Elijah calling Elisha:

[1 KINGS 19:19-20 KJV] "19 SO HE DEPARTED THENCE, AND FOUND ELISHA THE SON OF SHAPHAT, WHO [WAS] PLOWING [WITH] TWELVE YOKE [OF OXEN] BEFORE HIM, AND HE WITH THE TWELFTH: AND ELIJAH PASSED BY HIM, AND CAST HIS MANTLE UPON HIM. 20 AND HE LEFT THE OXEN, AND RAN AFTER ELIJAH, AND SAID, LET ME, I PRAY THEE, KISS MY FATHER AND MY MOTHER, AND [THEN] I WILL FOLLOW THEE. AND HE SAID UNTO HIM, GO BACK AGAIN: FOR WHAT HAVE I DONE TO THEE?"

At first, Elisha hesitated when Elijah called him to become his disciple and told him that he needed to kiss his father and mother goodbye first. Elisha wasn't saying that he needed to give them a goodbye kiss. This phrase is a Hebrew idiom for "Let me wait until my parents die and then I will follow you." We see a similar example in the New Testament when Jesus called someone to follow Him:

[LUKE 9:59-60 KJV] "59 AND HE SAID UNTO ANOTHER, FOLLOW ME. BUT HE SAID, LORD, SUFFER ME FIRST TO GO AND BURY MY FATHER. 60 JESUS SAID UNTO HIM, LET THE DEAD BURY THEIR DEAD: BUT GO THOU AND PREACH THE KINGDOM OF GOD."

Once you say yes to the call of God upon your life, then you can move forward without impediment and then you will hear the voice of God in the midst of the fire. Moses passed the test with flying colors and then God spoke to him:

*[EXODUS 3:14 KJV] "14 AND GOD SAID UNTO
MOSES, I AM THAT I AM: AND HE SAID, THUS
SHALT THOU SAY UNTO THE CHILDREN OF ISRAEL,
I AM HATH SENT ME UNTO YOU."*

Once you demonstrate that you are willing to go all the way with God, He will then speak to you and reveal His mission for your life for the sake of the burdens of others.

THE FIRE OF GOD FELL

[1 KINGS 18:1, 19, 21-39 KJV] "1 AND IT CAME TO PASS [AFTER] MANY DAYS, THAT THE WORD OF THE LORD CAME TO ELIJAH IN THE THIRD YEAR, SAYING, GO, SHEW THYSELF UNTO AHAB; AND I WILL SEND RAIN UPON THE EARTH. ... 19 NOW THEREFORE SEND, [AND] GATHER TO ME ALL ISRAEL UNTO MOUNT CARMEL, AND THE PROPHETS OF BAAL FOUR HUNDRED AND FIFTY, AND THE PROPHETS OF THE GROVES FOUR HUNDRED, WHICH EAT AT JEZEBEL'S TABLE. ... 21 AND ELIJAH CAME UNTO ALL THE PEOPLE, AND SAID, HOW LONG HALT YE BETWEEN TWO OPINIONS? IF THE LORD [BE] GOD, FOLLOW HIM: BUT IF BAAL, [THEN] FOLLOW HIM. AND THE PEOPLE ANSWERED HIM NOT A WORD. 22 THEN SAID ELIJAH UNTO THE PEOPLE, I, [EVEN] I ONLY, REMAIN A PROPHET OF THE LORD; BUT BAAL'S PROPHETS [ARE] FOUR HUNDRED AND FIFTY MEN. 23 LET THEM THEREFORE GIVE US TWO BULLOCKS; AND LET THEM CHOOSE ONE BULLOCK FOR THEMSELVES, AND CUT IT IN PIECES, AND LAY [IT] ON WOOD, AND PUT NO FIRE

[UNDER]: AND I WILL DRESS THE OTHER BULLOCK, AND LAY [IT] ON WOOD, AND PUT NO FIRE [UNDER]: 24 AND CALL YE ON THE NAME OF YOUR GODS, AND I WILL CALL ON THE NAME OF THE LORD: AND THE GOD THAT ANSWERETH BY FIRE, LET HIM BE GOD. AND ALL THE PEOPLE ANSWERED AND SAID, IT IS WELL SPOKEN. 25 AND ELIJAH SAID UNTO THE PROPHETS OF BAAL, CHOOSE YOU ONE BULLOCK FOR YOURSELVES, AND DRESS [IT] FIRST; FOR YE [ARE] MANY; AND CALL ON THE NAME OF YOUR GODS, BUT PUT NO FIRE [UNDER]. 26 AND THEY TOOK THE BULLOCK WHICH WAS GIVEN THEM, AND THEY DRESSED [IT], AND CALLED ON THE NAME OF BAAL FROM MORNING EVEN UNTIL NOON, SAYING, O BAAL, HEAR US. BUT [THERE WAS] NO VOICE, NOR ANY THAT ANSWERED. AND THEY LEAPED UPON THE ALTAR WHICH WAS MADE. 27 AND IT CAME TO PASS AT NOON, THAT ELIJAH MOCKED THEM, AND SAID, CRY ALOUD: FOR HE [IS] A GOD; EITHER HE IS TALKING, OR HE IS PURSUING, OR HE IS IN A JOURNEY, [OR] PERADVENTURE HE SLEEPETH, AND MUST BE AWAKED. 28 AND THEY CRIED ALOUD, AND CUT THEMSELVES AFTER THEIR MANNER WITH KNIVES AND LANCETS, TILL THE

BLOOD GUSHED OUT UPON THEM. 29 AND IT CAME TO PASS, WHEN MIDDAY WAS PAST, AND THEY PROPHESIED UNTIL THE [TIME] OF THE OFFERING OF THE [EVENING] SACRIFICE, THAT [THERE WAS] NEITHER VOICE, NOR ANY TO ANSWER, NOR ANY THAT REGARDED. 30 AND ELIJAH SAID UNTO ALL THE PEOPLE, COME NEAR UNTO ME. AND ALL THE PEOPLE CAME NEAR UNTO HIM. AND HE REPAIRED THE ALTAR OF THE LORD [THAT WAS] BROKEN DOWN. 31 AND ELIJAH TOOK TWELVE STONES, ACCORDING TO THE NUMBER OF THE TRIBES OF THE SONS OF JACOB, UNTO WHOM THE WORD OF THE LORD CAME, SAYING, ISRAEL SHALL BE THY NAME: 32 AND WITH THE STONES HE BUILT AN ALTAR IN THE NAME OF THE LORD: AND HE MADE A TRENCH ABOUT THE ALTAR, AS GREAT AS WOULD CONTAIN TWO MEASURES OF SEED. 33 AND HE PUT THE WOOD IN ORDER, AND CUT THE BULLOCK IN PIECES, AND LAID [HIM] ON THE WOOD, AND SAID, FILL FOUR BARRELS WITH WATER, AND POUR [IT] ON THE BURNT SACRIFICE, AND ON THE WOOD. 34 AND HE SAID, DO [IT] THE SECOND TIME. AND THEY DID [IT] THE SECOND TIME. AND HE SAID, DO [IT] THE THIRD TIME. AND THEY DID

[IT] THE THIRD TIME. 35 AND THE WATER RAN ROUND ABOUT THE ALTAR; AND HE FILLED THE TRENCH ALSO WITH WATER. 36 AND IT CAME TO PASS AT [THE TIME OF] THE OFFERING OF THE [EVENING] SACRIFICE, THAT ELIJAH THE PROPHET CAME NEAR, AND SAID, LORD GOD OF ABRAHAM, ISAAC, AND OF ISRAEL, LET IT BE KNOWN THIS DAY THAT THOU [ART] GOD IN ISRAEL, AND [THAT] I [AM] THY SERVANT, AND [THAT] I HAVE DONE ALL THESE THINGS AT THY WORD. 37 HEAR ME, O LORD, HEAR ME, THAT THIS PEOPLE MAY KNOW THAT THOU [ART] THE LORD GOD, AND [THAT] THOU HAST TURNED THEIR HEART BACK AGAIN. 38 THEN THE FIRE OF THE LORD FELL, AND CONSUMED THE BURNT SACRIFICE, AND THE WOOD, AND THE STONES, AND THE DUST, AND LICKED UP THE WATER THAT [WAS] IN THE TRENCH. 39 AND WHEN ALL THE PEOPLE SAW [IT], THEY FELL ON THEIR FACES: AND THEY SAID, THE LORD, HE [IS] THE GOD; THE LORD, HE [IS] THE GOD."

Elijah's challenge was the ultimate test for the sanctification of God's Name. The Hebrew words for this concept are, Kiddush Hashem.

The challenge was to demonstrate whether the God of Israel was God or if Baal was God. Elijah fearlessly took on the job of sanctifying God's Name by challenging 450 prophets of Baal. Counting the 400 prophets of Ashtarte, there were a total of 850 idolatrous prophets present at the duel. Elijah's goal was to demonstrate that only the God of Israel, the God of Abraham, Isaac, and Jacob was the true God and also to cause the Israelites and their wicked leader, King Ahab to return to Him. King Ahab and his infamous wife, Jezebel had led the Northern Kingdom of Israel astray into forsaking God and serving idols. Elijah was greatly outnumbered and statistically, the odds were against him: 850 to 1. They met at Mount Carmel for the challenge. This was spiritual warfare in its highest form. Not only was Elijah challenging the religious system, he was also taking on the corrupt political system that was led by Ahab and Jezebel. Elijah's ultimate test was to sanctify God's Name. Imagine an entire nation present to witness this duel between the forces of good and evil. The famine in the land was a reflection of the spiritual condition in the land. The Kingdom had forsaken the Lord God of Israel. With the entire nation present, Elijah called upon the people to gather around him. Elijah built an altar of 12 stones. The 12 stones symbolized the number of Israelite tribes. He then ordered that a wide trench be dug around it. After completing the preparation with the bullock for the sacrifice and the pouring of water on it and on the wood, he called upon the Name of the Lord. He prayed that the Israelites would turn their hearts back to Him. That was the entire purpose of this Kiddush Hashem, to turn the hearts of the people back to God. As soon as he finished praying, a flame of fire came down from God and consumed the offering, the wood, and the stones. Even the water was consumed. When the people saw it, they declared that the Lord is God. Elijah then slew the prophets of Baal. What a tremendous Kiddush Hashem!

Sometimes God will wait to reveal Himself to you when you step out in order to perform a Kiddush Hashem. Are you willing to step out for righteousness sake? Then only will the fire from God fall upon your situation. The fire of God falling on your situation can be an answer to your prayer. The book, <u>Rees Howell Intercessor</u> demonstrates how he constrained the fire of God for the widows in India. The Lord gave Reese Howell a burden for the child widows of India. Let's read an excerpt from the book:

"LORD ALSO GAVE HIM THE OFFER OF CONTINUING IN A HIDDEN MINISTRY FOR ANOTHER FOUR MONTHS TO GAIN SOME OTHER PLACES OF INTERCESSION, ONE BEING FOR THE CHILD WIDOWS OF INDIA WHOSE SUFFERINGS WERE SO GREAT UNDER THE PREVAILING SYSTEM. ... THE LORD THEN POINTED OUT TO REES THAT THESE WIDOWS WERE LIVING ON ONLY A HANDFUL OF RICE A DAY, AND REMINDED HIM OF THE LAW OF INTERCESSION, THAT BEFORE HE COULD INTERCEDE FOR THEM HE MUST LIVE LIKE THEM. SO HIS DIET WAS TO BE ONE MEAL OF OATS (PORRIDGE) EVERY TWO DAYS, ..."[v]

Rees took on the burden of the child widows. He continued this consecration for 10 weeks. He gained the victory for the child widows in 10 days. He carried out this consecration through the leading of the Lord. Elijah had also carried out his Kiddush Hashem through the leading of the Lord. Reese Howell constrained the fire of God over the unjust situation by eating like the child widows of India.

It took ten days to get the victory. With the independence and new Constitution of India in 1989, a legal change took place providing inheritance for the benefit of widows. Do you see how Reese performed a Kiddush Hashem for the widows and God honored his obedience by sending down fire from heaven by repairing the injustice to the widows of India? Now let's look at another example of the fire of God being constrained upon a situation in the ministry of the prophet, Elijah.

THE CAPTAIN OF FIFTY

Elijah was used by God to perform a Kiddush Hashem during the reign of King Ahaziah after the death of King Ahab:

[2 KINGS 1:1-2 KJV] "1 THEN MOAB REBELLED AGAINST ISRAEL AFTER THE DEATH OF AHAB. 2 AND AHAZIAH FELL DOWN THROUGH A LATTICE IN HIS UPPER CHAMBER THAT [WAS] IN SAMARIA, AND WAS SICK: AND HE SENT MESSENGERS, AND SAID UNTO THEM, GO, ENQUIRE OF BAALZEBUB THE GOD OF EKRON WHETHER I SHALL RECOVER OF THIS DISEASE."

Instead of consulting with a prophet of God, the king chose to consult with an idol to find out if he was going to recover of his injury. The Lord God sent Elijah once again to perform a Kiddush Hashem. The Lord gave Elijah a prophetic word telling him that Ahaziah was going to die because he failed to sanctify God's Name:

[2 KINGS 1:3-4 KJV] "3 BUT THE ANGEL OF THE LORD SAID TO ELIJAH THE TISHBITE, ARISE, GO UP TO MEET THE MESSENGERS OF THE KING OF SAMARIA, AND SAY UNTO THEM, [IS IT] NOT BECAUSE [THERE IS] NOT A GOD IN ISRAEL, [THAT] YE GO TO ENQUIRE OF BAALZEBUB THE GOD OF EKRON? 4 NOW THEREFORE THUS SAITH THE LORD, THOU SHALT NOT COME DOWN FROM THAT BED ON WHICH THOU ART GONE UP, BUT SHALT SURELY DIE. AND ELIJAH DEPARTED."

Elijah called down fire from Heaven upon two captains and their fifties:

[2 KINGS 1:10, 12, 14 KJV] "10 AND ELIJAH ANSWERED AND SAID TO THE CAPTAIN OF FIFTY, IF I [BE] A MAN OF GOD, THEN LET FIRE COME DOWN FROM HEAVEN, AND CONSUME THEE AND THY FIFTY. AND THERE CAME DOWN FIRE FROM HEAVEN, AND CONSUMED HIM AND HIS FIFTY. ... 12 AND ELIJAH ANSWERED AND SAID UNTO THEM, IF I [BE] A MAN OF GOD, LET FIRE COME DOWN FROM HEAVEN, AND CONSUME THEE AND THY

FIFTY. AND THE FIRE OF GOD CAME DOWN FROM HEAVEN, AND CONSUMED HIM AND HIS FIFTY. ... 14 BEHOLD, THERE CAME FIRE DOWN FROM HEAVEN, AND BURNT UP THE TWO CAPTAINS OF THE FORMER FIFTIES WITH THEIR FIFTIES: THEREFORE LET MY LIFE NOW BE PRECIOUS IN THY SIGHT."

The third captain and his fifty were spared from the fire. The Lord used Elijah to demonstrate that He alone is God. Following the move of God in the fire requires that we be willing to sanctify His Name even in the presence of kings. Often the fire of God will follow our obedience. God will be sanctified in the midst of the fire.

CHANUKAH

I would like to introduce you to another Biblical
feast to demonstrate the fire of God. This feast
is known as Chanukah. Chanukah is a minor
feast. It was not inaugurated by Moses in
Levicitus 23 like the major feasts. It was
instituted by the Rabbis. The first Chanukah
took place on 25th day of Kislev (9th month on the
Hebrew calendar). The Maccabees restored the
Temple in Jerusalem after defeating the armies
of the Syrian-Greek king, Antiochus IV.
Antiochus IV was a ruthless king who forced
Hellenistic beliefs and practices upon the Jews.
He attempted to uproot Jewish beliefs and
practices from the Jews. The Jews accepted the
Hellenistic way of life starting in 200 BC. Jewish
Hellenists helped Antiochus accomplish his goal
of wiping out the Jewish religion but they were
not successful. The Jewish Hellenists were in an
apathetic state and they had consequently given
into apathy. We too must eliminate apathy and
compromise in our lives. Apathy and
compromise quench the fire of God in our lives.
Josephus said the city of Jerusalem was handed
to the enemy without resistance. They were
worn out from the warfare and they easily
conceded to the compromise. Let's resist
Hellenistic ways in our culture and adopt a
Torah-centric way of life. This will ensure that

we walk in victory. Antiochus IV desecrated the Altar by sacrificing a pig upon it in 175 BC. The Temple was dedicated to the worship of Zeus. The Jews were forced to bow before it under the penalty of death. The Temple was completely desecrated. Antiochus IV proclaimed himself a god, taking the name Epiphanes—God manifest. The holiest place on earth was desecrated. The fearless Maccabees supernaturally fought and defeated the Syrian-Greeks and regained control of the Temple. According to one estimate, 6,000 Jews defeated 47,000 Syrian-Greek troops. This was a battle to restore the Presence of God in the Temple. The focus should not only be on the few defeating the many although it was a miracle of epic proportion. The focus should also be on restoring the Presence of the Lord in the Temple. After the Maccabees regained the Temple, they only had enough oil to keep the Temple's menorah lit for one day. They found only one small cruse of ritually pure olive oil. They needed 8 days to produce more of this type of oil. Another miracle then took place. Miraculously, the one-day's supply of oil burned for 8 days until the new oil could be made. Consequently, the Sages instituted the 8-day festival of Chanukah in order to commemorate the miracle of the multiplication of the oil. This supernatural fire represented the moving of the Lord in the Temple. The Lord honored the sacrifices of the Maccabees. The battle wasn't won when the Maccabees defeated

the Syrian-Greek tyrants. The battle was won
when worship was restored in the Temple.
Your body is a temple of the Holy Spirit:

*[1 CORINTHIANS 6:19 KJV] "19 WHAT? KNOW YE
NOT THAT YOUR BODY IS THE TEMPLE OF THE
HOLY GHOST [WHICH IS] IN YOU, WHICH YE HAVE
OF GOD, AND YE ARE NOT YOUR OWN?"*

CHAPTER 5 - WIND & FIRE

In this chapter, I will describe moves of God that included the wind and fire. The manifestation of the wind and fire is represented by the feast of Shavuot or Pentecost. They are both the same feast. Shavuot is the Hebrew name for the feast meaning Weeks. Pentecost is the Greek name for the feast meaning Fiftieth. We encounter the wind and the fire in the feast of Shavuot.

THE HOUSE WAS FILLED

[ACTS 2:2-3 KJV] "2 AND SUDDENLY THERE CAME A SOUND FROM HEAVEN AS OF A RUSHING MIGHTY WIND, AND IT FILLED ALL THE HOUSE WHERE THEY WERE SITTING. 3 AND THERE APPEARED UNTO THEM CLOVEN TONGUES LIKE AS OF FIRE, AND IT SAT UPON EACH OF THEM."

The Holy Spirit descended into the Upper Room upon the 120 that were present. The Holy Spirit moved into the room in the wind and fire. This manifestation of the Holy Spirit occurred on Pentecost. The church was born on Pentecost. Countless Jews were present in Jerusalem on this day because it was a major feast. This day wasn't the first Shavuot. The first Shavuot occurred when the Israelites received the 10 Commandments at Mount Sinai. Israel became a nation on Shavuot. The day we call Pentecost is the anniversary of the day in which God gave the Ten Commandments to Israel.

ISRAEL BECOMES A NATION

On the first Shavuot, the Israelites became a nation. On the fiftieth day of their journey out of Egypt, they received the Ten Commandments at the foot of Mount Sinai.

[EXODUS 19:20 KJV] "20 AND THE LORD CAME DOWN UPON MOUNT SINAI, ON THE TOP OF THE MOUNT: AND THE LORD CALLED MOSES [UP] TO THE TOP OF THE MOUNT; AND MOSES WENT UP."

How did the Presence of God descend? He bent down the upper heavens and He spread them upon the mountain like a sheet on a bed, and the Throne of Glory descended upon them. I will describe the Throne of God in detail when study Elijah's ascent. At the "Giving of the Torah," a "meetings of worlds" took place. The physical world as it stands embraced the spiritual realm. The Israelites broke loose from the world and embraced a higher, spiritual reality. They experienced the freedom from sin that Adam and Eve knew before the Fall in the Garden of Eden. They experienced a level of holiness that even exceeded the level of holiness achieved by Adam and Eve in the Garden of Eden.

SHEMOS 20:15 "ALL THE PEOPLE COULD SEE THE SOUNDS (WHICH GOD SPOKE), THE TORCHES, THE SOUND OF THE SHOFAR, AND THE SMOKING MOUNTAIN. THE PEOPLE SAW AND THEY TREMBLED AND THEY WITHDREW BACKWARDS (THE FULL LENGTH OF THE CAMP).

The people could see the sounds. This sounds like a mistake in the text. How can people see sounds? This is no mistake. The Lord had elevated the senses of the Israelites. The people had been lifted out of their normal, earthly perspective. They were now more in tune with the realm of the Spirit and their physical senses became blurred. God first spoke all the commandments with one utterance in a crescendo of sound. The Sages say:

"THE WORLD WAS MUTE, AS THE VOICE PROCLAIMED, "I AM THE LORD YOUR GOD ..."

" TO THAT VOICE, THE MIDRASH CONTINUES, THERE WAS NO ECHO. IT SOUNDED ALONE IN A SILENT WORLD THAT HUMANITY MIGHT KNOW THERE IS NONE OTHER BESIDE HIM. THIS, SAYS SCRIPTURE, WAS "A GREAT VOICE," FOR THE MIDRASH IT MEANS: "AND IT WENT ON NO MORE" - NO ECHO EXTENDED IT. THE PHRASE COULD MEAN: "AND IT DID NOT END." THAT GREAT VOICE INDEED DID NOT STOP THEN; AN ECHO HAD REVERBERATED AND RESOUNDED THEREAFTER FROM SINAI, DAY AFTER DAY, CALLING OUT."

The Talmud (Shabbat 88b) states the following in regards to the Mount Sinai experience at the receiving of the 10 Commandments:

- 60,000 angels came down upon Mt. Sinai with 2 crowns each.

- 120,000 crowns were given to the Israelites. (Do you see the parallels to Pentecost? There were 120 people in the Upper Room).

- One crown represented that we will hear/see

- The other crown represents that we will obey.

- 22,000 chariots of angels appeared on Mt Sinai which parallel the 22 are letters in the Hebrew Aleph-Beit.

When Messiah comes, our senses will be elevated to this level. Come Messiah, Come!

ELIJAH'S ASCENT

Elijah again encountered the Voice of God. This time it was in the form of the wind and fire. Elijah told his servant, Elisha that he would receive a double-portion of his anointing if he saw him taken away. Elijah wasn't saying that Elisha needed to physically see what was happening. He was telling him that he needed to comprehend the spiritual experience he was about to encounter:

[2 KINGS 2:9-10 KJV] "9 AND IT CAME TO PASS, WHEN THEY WERE GONE OVER, THAT ELIJAH SAID UNTO ELISHA, ASK WHAT I SHALL DO FOR THEE, BEFORE I BE TAKEN AWAY FROM THEE. AND ELISHA SAID, I PRAY THEE, LET A DOUBLE PORTION OF THY SPIRIT BE UPON ME. 10 AND HE SAID, THOU HAST ASKED A HARD THING: [NEVERTHELESS], IF THOU SEE ME [WHEN I AM] TAKEN FROM THEE, IT SHALL BE SO UNTO THEE; BUT IF NOT, IT SHALL NOT BE [SO]."

As they went on and talked about Torah, they encountered the chariot and horses of fire and Elijah went up in a whirlwind:

[2 KINGS 2:11 KJV] "11 AND IT CAME TO PASS, AS THEY STILL WENT ON, AND TALKED, THAT, BEHOLD, [THERE APPEARED] A CHARIOT OF FIRE, AND HORSES OF FIRE, AND PARTED THEM BOTH ASUNDER; AND ELIJAH WENT UP BY A WHIRLWIND INTO HEAVEN."

What did Elisha see? Seeing and perceiving were the prerequisites to receiving the double-portion anointing. Elisha perceived the throne of God and its angels in the heavenly encounter.

THE HEAVENLY CHARIOT OF WIND AND FIRE

[EZEKIEL 1:4 KJV] "4 AND I LOOKED, AND, BEHOLD, A WHIRLWIND CAME OUT OF THE NORTH, A GREAT CLOUD, AND A FIRE INFOLDING ITSELF, AND A BRIGHTNESS [WAS] ABOUT IT, AND OUT OF THE MIDST THEREOF AS THE COLOUR OF AMBER, OUT OF THE MIDST OF THE FIRE."

EZEKIEL 1:4 (ARTSCROLL EZEKIEL) THEN I LOOKED AND BEHOLD! A STORMY WIND WAS COMING FROM THE NORTH, A GREAT CLOUD WITH FLASHING FIRE AND A BRILLIANCE SURROUND IT; AND FROM ITS MIDST CAME A SEMBLANCE OF CHASMAL FROM THE MIDST OF THE FIRE.[5]

There were countless prophets in the days of Elijah but only Elisha was found worthy to carry on his mission. Elisha encountered the chariot of God's glory. Elisha saw the Chariot (Merkavah) of the Glory (Shechinah) when

127

Elijah was taken up by the whirlwind. I will do my best to explain this revelation. The depth of Elisha's experience is beyond my comprehension. The chariot of God's glory includes many species of angels. According to Maimonides, there are 10 ranks of angels. He said that all angels fall under 1 of 10 ranks. These ranks refer to the degree of the angels' comprehension of God. We can apply this to our lives. Every one of us has a different comprehension of God and His ways. Our comprehension will determine the depth in which we can be used by God. One of the rewards of Torah study is the gift of greater comprehension of God and His ways. May the Lord grant all of us a greater depth of understanding. These 10 ranks are listed as follows: [67]

1. Chayot Hakodesh
2. Ophanim
3. Erelim
4. Chashmalim
5. Seraphim
6. Malachim
7. Elokim
8. Bene Elokim
9. Cheruvim
10. Ishim

The first rank of angels is the Chayot Hakodesh which are known as the Holy Living Ones. I believe these species of angels are seen as the whirlwind in Ezekiel 1:4:

[EZEKIEL 1:4 KJV] "4 AND I LOOKED, AND, BEHOLD, A WHIRLWIND CAME OUT OF THE NORTH, ..."

The second rank of angels is the Ophanim. We see the Ophanim in Ezekiel 1:15:

[EZEKIEL 1:15 KJV] "15 NOW AS I BEHELD THE LIVING CREATURES, BEHOLD ONE WHEEL UPON THE EARTH BY THE LIVING CREATURES, WITH HIS FOUR FACES."

The Ophanim are the wheels of the chariot. They were below each Chayot but they were not attached to the feet of the "Chayot" angels. These angels are shaped like wheels. These wheel angels are described as "a wheel inside of a wheel." Ophanim literally translates as wheels, cycles, or ways. The cycles can refer to learning Torah through the annual Torah reading cycle and to the Hebrew feasts. Ophanim also means "to plan." The plan that is referred to by these angels is the plan that is drawn out in order to prepare them for a real action. Likewise, in our walk with the Lord, we must prepare a plan for every assignment God gives us.

The third species of angels is known as the Erelim. Erelim means Brave Ones. They are described in Isaiah 33:7:

[ISAIAH 33:7 KJV] "7 BEHOLD, THEIR VALIANT ONES SHALL CRY WITHOUT: THE AMBASSADORS OF PEACE SHALL WEEP BITTERLY." THIS DIVINE LIGHT IS THE REALIZATION OF G-D'S ACTION IN THE SPIRITUAL WORLD, WHILE IT HAS YET TO BE MATERIALIZED IN THE PHYSICAL WORLD.

The fourth species of angels is known as the Chashmalim. Chashmalim means Glowing ones or Amber ones. They are described in Ezekiel 1:4:

[EZEKIEL 1:4 KJV] "4 AND I LOOKED, AND, BEHOLD, A WHIRLWIND CAME OUT OF THE

NORTH, A GREAT CLOUD, AND A FIRE INFOLDING ITSELF, AND A BRIGHTNESS [WAS] ABOUT IT, AND OUT OF THE MIDST THEREOF AS THE COLOUR OF AMBER, OUT OF THE MIDST OF THE FIRE." REFERS TO A GLITTERING SUBSTANCE. THEY REFLECT DIVINE LIGHT.

The fifth species of angels are known as the Seraphim. Seraphim means Burning Ones. They are described in Isaiah 6:2-3 and Revelation 4:8:

[ISAIAH 6:2-3 KJV] "2 ABOVE IT STOOD THE SERAPHIMS: EACH ONE HAD SIX WINGS; WITH TWAIN HE COVERED HIS FACE, AND WITH TWAIN HE COVERED HIS FEET, AND WITH TWAIN HE DID FLY. 3 AND ONE CRIED UNTO ANOTHER, AND SAID, HOLY, HOLY, HOLY, [IS] THE LORD OF HOSTS: THE WHOLE EARTH [IS] FULL OF HIS GLORY."

[REVELATION 4:8 KJV] "8 AND THE FOUR BEASTS HAD EACH OF THEM SIX WINGS ABOUT [HIM]; AND [THEY WERE] FULL OF EYES WITHIN: AND THEY REST NOT DAY AND NIGHT, SAYING, HOLY, HOLY, HOLY, LORD GOD ALMIGHTY, WHICH WAS, AND IS, AND IS TO COME."

These angels appear like flashes of fire continuously ascending and descending. These "Seraphim" angels empowers the movement of the chariot. These angels absorb the light that is reflected from the Chashmalim. The word, saraph can mean to absorb a substance. These angels absorb the remainder of the divine light in order to transfer it to the next level of angels. In the hierarchy of these angels, "Seraphim" are the highest, that is, closest to God, followed by the "Chayot", which are followed by the "Ophanim." The chariot is in a constant state of motion, and the energy behind this movement runs according to this hierarchy. The movement of the "Ophanim" is controlled by the "Chayot" while the movement of the "Chayot" is controlled by the "Seraphim". The Seraphim are described as flashes of lightning in Ezekiel 1. The movement of all the angels of the chariot are controlled by the "Likeness of a Man" on the Throne.

Isaiah and Ezekiel both saw the King who is called the "Likeness of a Man." I believe the "Likeness of a Man" is referring to the Messiah. He is the one stands in the heavenly chariot. Both the prophets Isaiah and Ezekiel had the same vision of the heavenly chariot but each described it differently. Here is an explanation why the visions are described differently per Orthodox Union: "The people of Isaiah's generation were like citizens who reside in a kingdom's capital, while those of Ezekiel's generation were like townspeople who reside in a distant village. When a resident of the capital says, "I saw the king today," his neighbors will reply, "You did? That's nice." They don't need elaboration because they're used to seeing the castle, the king's carriage, etc. But when a villager sees the king, it's an uncommon experience. His neighbors want to know all about the king's appearance, his armor, his horse, and more. This is the reason why Ezekiel's description of his Heavenly vision is so much more detailed than Isaiah's."[8] Isaiah was a city dweller and Ezekiel was a village dweller. Ezekiel needed to use more detail to describe the vision to the villagers. Isaiah's audience were city dwellers that were already familiar with the concept of kingship and didn't need the painstaking details.

The sixth species of angels are known as the Malachim. Malachim means Messengers or angels. I believe the following scriptures in Hebrews and Luke describe the Malachim.

[HEBREWS 1:7, 14 KJV] "7 AND OF THE ANGELS HE SAITH, WHO MAKETH HIS ANGELS SPIRITS, AND HIS MINISTERS A FLAME OF FIRE. ... 14 ARE THEY NOT ALL MINISTERING SPIRITS, SENT FORTH TO MINISTER FOR THEM WHO SHALL BE HEIRS OF SALVATION?"

[LUKE 22:43 KJV] "43 AND THERE APPEARED AN ANGEL UNTO HIM FROM HEAVEN, STRENGTHENING HIM."

[LUKE 2:9-11 KJV] "9 AND, LO, THE ANGEL OF THE LORD CAME UPON THEM, AND THE GLORY OF THE LORD SHONE ROUND ABOUT THEM: AND THEY WERE SORE AFRAID. 10 AND THE ANGEL SAID UNTO THEM, FEAR NOT: FOR, BEHOLD, I BRING YOU GOOD TIDINGS OF GREAT JOY, WHICH

SHALL BE TO ALL PEOPLE. 11 FOR UNTO YOU IS BORN THIS DAY IN THE CITY OF DAVID A SAVIOUR, WHICH IS CHRIST THE LORD. "

[LUKE 2:13-14 KJV] "13 AND SUDDENLY THERE WAS WITH THE ANGEL A MULTITUDE OF THE HEAVENLY HOST PRAISING GOD, AND SAYING, 14 GLORY TO GOD IN THE HIGHEST, AND ON EARTH PEACE, GOOD WILL TOWARD MEN. "

The Malachim refer to teachers that are able to take a completely abstract concept and explain it. These angels are able to start the conversion process of a completely spiritual idea and begin its transformation into the physical world. This is also a quality that teachers must demonstrate when they teach their students.

The seventh species of angels are known as the Elokim. Elokim means Godly beings. Elokim doesn't always refer to God. Sometimes the word, Elokim refers to kings and rulers. According to Maimonides, these angels are similar to the physical rulers of the world. These are the angels that transfer an idea from the spiritual world into the physical world.

The eighth species of angels are known as the Bene Elokim. Bene Elokim means Sons of Godly Beings. Bene Elokim are the angels that guide the idea in the physical world. This is in order that the idea works in the way that it was intended to work. The Archangel Michael is part of this species of angels.

The ninth species of angels are known as the Cheruvim . The Cheruvim are the 4 chayot – living creatures that drive the chariot.

[EZEKIEL 1:5 KJV] "5 ALSO OUT OF THE MIDST THEREOF [CAME] THE LIKENESS OF FOUR LIVING CREATURES. AND THIS [WAS] THEIR APPEARANCE; THEY HAD THE LIKENESS OF A MAN."

EZEKIEL 1:5 [ARTSCROLL EZEKIEL] "AND FROM ITS MIDST, A SEMBLANCE OF FOUR CHAYOS. THIS WAS THEIR APPEARANCE: THEY HAD THE SEMBLANCE OF A MAN;"[1]

Each chayah (singular for chayot or chayos) has 4 faces (man, lion, ox, and eagle) on each side giving a total of 16 faces per Chayah. Each face has 4 wings so that each Chayah has 64 wings. The total number of faces and wings for all four Chayos are 64 faces and 256 wings. The positioning of the faces of chayot mirrors the 4 groupings of the Israelite tribes in the Wilderness:

- Camp of Reuben (man) with Gad, Shimon, and Reuben to the South.

- Camp of Judah (lion) with Judah, Issachar, and Zebulan to the East.

- Camp of Dan (eagle) with Dan, Asher, and Naphtali to the North.

- Camp of Ephraim (ox) with Benjamin, Mannaseh, and Ephraim to the West. Chayos means supporters - represents the highest assistants. The Archangel Gabriel is part of this specie of angels. The following picture shows the 4 groupings of Israelite tribes in the Wilderness. Note how the representation of each camp matches the four faces of each Cherub. The Camp of Judah is represented by the Lion. The Camp of Reuben is represented by the man. The camp of Ephraim is represented by the Ox.

The Camp of Dan is represented by the eagle.

The Desert Encampment

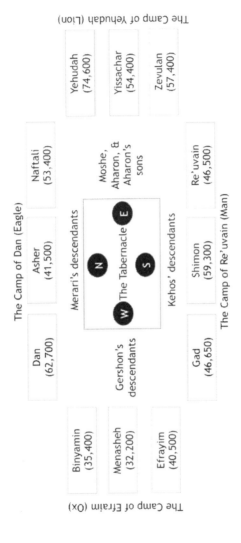

The Camp of Yehudah (Lion)

Yehudah (74,600)	
Yissachar (54,400)	
Zevulan (57,400)	

The Camp of Dan (Eagle)

Naftali (53,400)

Moshe, Aharon, & Aharon's sons

Re'uvain (46,500)

Asher (41,500)

Merari's descendants

N

E

W

The Tabernacle

S

Shimon (59,300)

The Camp of Re'uvain (Man)

Kehos' descendants

Dan (62,700)

Gershon's descendants

Gad (46,650)

Binyamin (35,400)

Menasheh (32,200)

Efrayim (40,500)

The Camp of Efraim (Ox)

140

The tenth species of angels are known as the Ishim. The Ishim are "manlike beings" similar to fires. See Genesis 18:2 and Daniel 10:5:

[GENESIS 18:2 KJV] "2 AND HE LIFT UP HIS EYES AND LOOKED, AND, LO, THREE MEN STOOD BY HIM: AND WHEN HE SAW [THEM], HE RAN TO MEET THEM FROM THE TENT DOOR, AND BOWED HIMSELF TOWARD THE GROUND,"

[DANIEL 10:5 KJV] "5 THEN I LIFTED UP MINE EYES, AND LOOKED, AND BEHOLD A CERTAIN MAN CLOTHED IN LINEN, WHOSE LOINS [WERE] GIRDED WITH FINE GOLD OF UPHAZ:"

The angel with the face of the man is always on the east side and looks up at the "Likeness of a Man" that drives the chariot. The "Likeness of a Man" sits on a throne made of sapphire.

The wind and the fire represent higher levels of spiritual comprehension. The Heavenly Chariot and its angels described in Ezekiel's and Isaiah's visions are probably one of the most difficult prophecies to comprehend in the Bible. Elisha had attained a lofty level of spiritual comprehension when Elijah was taken up by the whirlwind. It was only when Elisha perceived what was taking place that he received the double-portion of the spirit that was upon Elijah.

CHAPTER 6 – A STILL SMALL VOICE

BAT KOL "DAUGHTERS OF THE VOICE"

[1 KINGS 19:12-13 KJV] "12 AND AFTER THE EARTHQUAKE A FIRE; [BUT] THE LORD [WAS] NOT IN THE FIRE: AND AFTER THE FIRE A STILL SMALL VOICE. 13 AND IT WAS [SO], WHEN ELIJAH HEARD [IT], THAT HE WRAPPED HIS FACE IN HIS MANTLE, AND WENT OUT, AND STOOD IN THE ENTERING IN OF THE CAVE. AND, BEHOLD, [THERE CAME] A VOICE UNTO HIM, AND SAID, WHAT DOEST THOU HERE, ELIJAH?"

Elijah received such an awesome encounter with the Holy Spirit. This experience was greater than even the earthquake and the fire. I believe Elijah received a Holy of Holies type experience. He encountered the mercy of God. He experienced the love of God. He encountered the heart of God. He stood at the same cleft of the rock where Moses had encountered the "back parts" of God.

The fifth letter of the Aleph-Beit is Hei. This letter is barely heard and it alludes to God, Who manifests Himself in quietness. When the Lord spoke to Elijah in the Cleft of the Rock after the strong wind, earthquake, and fire, He revealed Himself with a soundless whisper which is represented by the letter, Hei.[15] Each letter of the Hebrew Aleph-Beit represents a manifestation of His Glory.

The Still, Small Voice in Hebrew is called a Bat Kol. It is the Divine voice of God. According to http://www.myjewishlearning.com/article/bat-kol-a-divine-voice/ the Bat Kol is considered the lowest level of prophecy. I am not yet convinced that it is the lowest form of Divine communication. I think it is the highest form of Divine communication and this is the method of communication that the Heavenly Father used to communicate with Jesus at least two times in the Gospels. It literally means "Daughters of the Voice." This term is given in Talmudic literature. It is a Divine communication from Heaven. Before we dive into the significance of the Bat Kol, I would like to give you some examples of the Bat Kol from the Gospels. Jesus was confirmed into ministry through the Bat Kol.

VOICE FROM HEAVEN

Jesus received a Bat Kol when He emerged from the waters of the Jordan after His baptism:

MATTHEW 3:17 (KJV) "AND LO A VOICE FROM HEAVEN, SAYING, THIS IS MY BELOVED SON, IN WHOM I AM WELL PLEASED."

Also, at the Mount of Transfiguration, the Heavenly Father spoke through the Bat Kol:

[MATTHEW 17:1-5 KJV] "1 AND AFTER SIX DAYS JESUS TAKETH PETER, JAMES, AND JOHN HIS BROTHER, AND BRINGETH THEM UP INTO AN HIGH MOUNTAIN APART, 2 AND WAS TRANSFIGURED BEFORE THEM: AND HIS FACE DID SHINE AS THE SUN, AND HIS RAIMENT WAS WHITE AS THE LIGHT. 3 AND, BEHOLD, THERE APPEARED UNTO THEM MOSES AND ELIAS TALKING WITH HIM. 4 THEN ANSWERED PETER, AND SAID UNTO JESUS, LORD,

IT IS GOOD FOR US TO BE HERE: IF THOU WILT, LET US MAKE HERE THREE TABERNACLES; ONE FOR THEE, AND ONE FOR MOSES, AND ONE FOR ELIAS. 5 WHILE HE YET SPAKE, BEHOLD, A BRIGHT CLOUD OVERSHADOWED THEM: AND BEHOLD A VOICE OUT OF THE CLOUD, WHICH SAID, THIS IS MY BELOVED SON, IN WHOM I AM WELL PLEASED; HEAR YE HIM."

ELIJAH HEARS A VOICE

[1 Kings 19:1-3 KJV] "1 And Ahab told Jezebel all that Elijah had done, and withal how he had slain all the prophets with the sword. 2 Then Jezebel sent a messenger unto Elijah, saying, So let the gods do [to me], and more also, if I make not thy life as the life of one of them by to morrow about this time. 3 And when he saw [that], he arose, and went for his life, and came to Beersheba, which [belongeth] to Judah, and left his servant there."

Elijah received the revelation of the Bat Kol at Mount Sinai (also known as Mount Horeb).

After slaying the prophets of Baal, Elijah fled to Mount Horeb. King Ahab told his wicked wife, Jezebel all that had taken place on Mount Carmel including the death of the prophets of Baal. Ahab expected Jezebel to agree that Elijah's miracles proved that he was God's true prophet. To his surprise, Jezebel burst into a rage and swore that she would do to Elijah what he had done to their false prophets. Elijah fled to the desert of Judah. There he sat down amongst the bushes in a mood of great disappointment. Doesn't this sound like Jonah after leading the Ninevites to repentance?

[1 KINGS 19:4-8 KJV] "4 BUT HE HIMSELF WENT A DAY'S JOURNEY INTO THE WILDERNESS, AND CAME AND SAT DOWN UNDER A JUNIPER TREE: AND HE REQUESTED FOR HIMSELF THAT HE MIGHT DIE; AND SAID, IT IS ENOUGH; NOW, O LORD, TAKE AWAY MY LIFE; FOR I [AM] NOT BETTER THAN MY FATHERS. 5 AND AS HE LAY AND SLEPT UNDER A JUNIPER TREE, BEHOLD, THEN AN ANGEL TOUCHED HIM, AND SAID UNTO HIM, ARISE [AND] EAT. 6 AND HE LOOKED, AND, BEHOLD, [THERE WAS] A CAKE BAKEN ON THE COALS, AND A CRUSE OF WATER AT HIS HEAD. AND HE DID EAT AND DRINK, AND LAID HIM DOWN

AGAIN. 7 AND THE ANGEL OF THE LORD CAME AGAIN THE SECOND TIME, AND TOUCHED HIM, AND SAID, ARISE [AND] EAT; BECAUSE THE JOURNEY [IS] TOO GREAT FOR THEE. 8 AND HE AROSE, AND DID EAT AND DRINK, AND WENT IN THE STRENGTH OF THAT MEAT FORTY DAYS AND FORTY NIGHTS UNTO HOREB THE MOUNT OF GOD."

He was wearied from his flight and he was hungry and thirsty. He lay down and fell asleep under a Juniper tree. The tree was also an angel in the disguise of a tree according to one of my readings. An angel touched him and told him to get up and eat. Elijah opened his eyes and saw a cruse of water and a cake next to him. He ate and drank and fell asleep for the second time. Again, an angel awoke him and said, "Arise [and] eat; because the journey [is] too great for thee." Elijah got up, ate, drank, and went on his journey. With the strength derived from that meal, he walked forty days and forty nights until he reached Mount Horeb. I would like a meal like that! He went 40 days and nights without food and drink. Moses had also gone 40 days and nights without food on several occasions. Jesus went 40 days without food and drink when the Spirit of God led Him into the Wilderness:

[MATTHEW 4:1 KJV] "1 THEN WAS JESUS LED UP OF THE SPIRIT INTO THE WILDERNESS TO BE TEMPTED OF THE DEVIL."

Elijah finally arrived at Mount Horeb. He took refuge in a cleft of a rock. The word of the Lord then came to Elijah and spoke to him:

[1 KINGS 19:9 KJV] "AND HE CAME THITHER UNTO A CAVE, AND LODGED THERE; AND, BEHOLD, THE WORD OF THE LORD [CAME] TO HIM, AND HE SAID UNTO HIM, WHAT DOEST THOU HERE, ELIJAH?"

What was this cleft of the rock? It was the same cleft of the rock that Moses came to when the Lord revealed His glory to him:

[EXODUS 33:22 KJV] "AND IT SHALL COME TO PASS, WHILE MY GLORY PASSETH BY, THAT I WILL PUT THEE IN A CLIFT OF THE ROCK, AND WILL COVER THEE WITH MY HAND WHILE I PASS BY:"

The reason why I bring in the example of God showing Moses His glory is because both experiences are similar. This is how Elijah responded to God's question:

[1 KINGS 19:10 KJV] "AND HE SAID, I HAVE BEEN VERY JEALOUS FOR THE LORD GOD OF HOSTS: FOR THE CHILDREN OF ISRAEL HAVE FORSAKEN THY COVENANT, THROWN DOWN THINE ALTARS, AND SLAIN THY PROPHETS WITH THE SWORD; AND I, [EVEN] I ONLY, AM LEFT; AND THEY SEEK MY LIFE, TO TAKE IT AWAY."

Elijah began by complaining about his suffering and about his zeal to protect the honor of God. This concept is known as Kiddush Hashem. He also mourned the loss of the true prophets of God and said that he was the only true prophet left and that they sought to take his life too. He also condemned the people of Israel in his response. The Midrash says that Elijah wanted God to punish Israel, but God said to him, "They abandoned My covenant, not yours; they dismantled My altars, not yours; they killed My prophets, not yours. Why are you more zealous than I?" Next, the Lord revealed Himself to Elijah in the Still, Small Voice:

[1 KINGS 19:11-14 KJV] "11 AND HE SAID, GO FORTH, AND STAND UPON THE MOUNT BEFORE THE LORD. AND, BEHOLD, THE LORD PASSED BY, AND A GREAT AND STRONG WIND RENT THE MOUNTAINS, AND BRAKE IN PIECES THE ROCKS BEFORE THE LORD; [BUT] THE LORD [WAS] NOT IN THE WIND: AND AFTER THE WIND AN EARTHQUAKE; [BUT] THE LORD [WAS] NOT IN THE EARTHQUAKE: 12 AND AFTER THE EARTHQUAKE A FIRE; [BUT] THE LORD [WAS] NOT IN THE FIRE: AND AFTER THE FIRE A STILL SMALL VOICE. 13 AND IT WAS [SO], WHEN ELIJAH HEARD [IT], THAT HE WRAPPED HIS FACE IN HIS MANTLE, AND WENT OUT, AND STOOD IN THE ENTERING IN OF THE CAVE. AND, BEHOLD, [THERE CAME] A VOICE UNTO HIM, AND SAID, WHAT DOEST THOU HERE, ELIJAH? 14 AND HE SAID, I HAVE BEEN VERY JEALOUS FOR THE LORD GOD OF HOSTS: BECAUSE THE CHILDREN OF ISRAEL HAVE FORSAKEN THY COVENANT, THROWN DOWN THINE ALTARS, AND SLAIN THY PROPHETS

WITH THE SWORD; AND I, [EVEN] I ONLY, AM
LEFT; AND THEY SEEK MY LIFE, TO TAKE IT
AWAY."

God rebuked Elijah through a demonstration of a strong wind, an earthquake, a fire, and then a still small voice to show Elijah that He was far from punishing the Israelites. He showed Elijah that He was patient, compassionate, and gives His people time to repent. Elijah should have understood God's ways and he should have been interceding for the people and not attacking them. Using an American idiomatic phrase, Elijah threw the people of Israel under the bus.⁹ God told Elijah to go and stand upon the mount. This was an implied rebuke because this is the same place where Moses stood after the Israelites committed the sin with the Golden Calf. Despite the gravity of their sin, Moses still pleaded for God's mercy upon Israel and he successfully obtained God's mercy. Elijah, in contrast, wanted the people to be punished for their sins. Consequently, God now told him, he should not remain in Moses' place. God told him to stand on the mountain-side. God manifested Himself to him. As Elijah stood on the mountain-side, God manifested Himself to him. First, a strong wind blew but God was not in the wind. Second, a strong earthquake came but God was not in the earthquake either.

Third, there came a fire, but God was not in the fire. Elijah discerned that God was not in the wind, the earthquake, and the fire. Elijah knew that angels guided such powerful forces such as the wind, earthquakes, and fire. We often blame God for natural disasters that take place in the earth. For example, we should not blame God for the disasters that take place in the earth such as Hurricanes Harvey and Maria that took place in 2017.

Finally, Elijah heard a still small voice. He covered his face and stood at the entrance of the cleft of the rock. He recognized that God was present in the still small voice. This voice is also known as a still, thin voice. According to Ralbag,[10] the still, thin voice is a cross between silence and sound. This voice symbolized that if God's people failed to understand that difficult economic times had come upon them because of their downward spiral into sin. God didn't want to bring punishment upon them. This Still Small Voice was a response to sin but it was still and thin. This meant that if the people chose to ignore God's voice, then they would not hear him. As you look at the books toward to the end of the Tanakh, you will see that the books get shorter and shorter. The books of the Trei Asar[11] "The Twelve" are much shorter than the other books of the Tanakh. Christians refer to the Trei Asar as the 12 Minor Prophets. There is nothing minor about the 12 Minor Prophets. The books of Trei Asar, Hosea through Malachi are just much shorter than the other books of Nevi'im (prophecy). I believe this was because the people had built a resistance to hearing and obeying God's voice and as a result, the books become shorter.

God's voice came to Elijah again. God then commissioned Elijah for the last part of his ministry. This commissioning included anointing Hazael as king over Syria, anointing Jehu as king over Israel, and finally anointing Elisha to replace him as prophet in his place. I don't believe that Elijah passed the test that the Lord set before him. We don't read about Elijah interceding for the Israelites. In contrast, his servant, Jonah showed compassion to the Israelites. He chose to flee from God's presence rather than to put the lives of the Israelites in danger of the pending Assyrian exile. Moses demonstrated a quality that Elijah lacked. When the Israelites sinned with the Golden Calf (Chet HaEgel), Moses interceded for them. He went as far as requesting that he be blotted out of the Book of Life if He would not forgive Israel:

[EXODUS 32:31-32 KJV] "31 AND MOSES RETURNED UNTO THE LORD, AND SAID, OH, THIS PEOPLE HAVE SINNED A GREAT SIN, AND HAVE MADE THEM GODS OF GOLD. 32 YET NOW, IF

THOU WILT FORGIVE THEIR SIN--; AND IF NOT, BLOT ME, I PRAY THEE, OUT OF THY BOOK WHICH THOU HAST WRITTEN."

Imagine having Moses as your leader. He was a leader that was truly concerned for the welfare of his people. He put them above himself.

SHOW ME YOUR GLORY

Moses requested that the Lord show him His glory:

[EXODUS 33:18-23 KJV] "18 AND HE SAID, I BESEECH THEE, SHEW ME THY GLORY. 19 AND HE SAID, I WILL MAKE ALL MY GOODNESS PASS BEFORE THEE, AND I WILL PROCLAIM THE NAME OF THE LORD BEFORE THEE; AND WILL BE GRACIOUS TO WHOM I WILL BE GRACIOUS, AND WILL SHEW MERCY ON WHOM I WILL SHEW MERCY. 20 AND HE SAID, THOU CANST NOT SEE MY FACE:

FOR THERE SHALL NO MAN SEE ME, AND LIVE. 21
AND THE LORD SAID, BEHOLD, [THERE IS] A
PLACE BY ME, AND THOU SHALT STAND UPON A
ROCK: 22 AND IT SHALL COME TO PASS, WHILE MY
GLORY PASSETH BY, THAT I WILL PUT THEE IN A
CLIFT OF THE ROCK, AND WILL COVER THEE WITH
MY HAND WHILE I PASS BY: 23 AND I WILL TAKE
AWAY MINE HAND, AND THOU SHALT SEE MY BACK
PARTS: BUT MY FACE SHALL NOT BE SEEN."

This cleft of the rock where God showed Moses
his glory is the same place where Elijah stood
when God spoke to Him. God was reminding
Elijah of His merciful nature by having him
stand in the same place that Moses stood. The
Lord revealed His ways to Moses which are His
merciful ways:

[EXODUS 34:6-8 KJV] "6 AND THE LORD
PASSED BY BEFORE HIM, AND PROCLAIMED, THE
LORD, THE LORD GOD, MERCIFUL AND
GRACIOUS, LONGSUFFERING, AND ABUNDANT IN
GOODNESS AND TRUTH, 7 KEEPING MERCY FOR
THOUSANDS, FORGIVING INIQUITY AND
TRANSGRESSION AND SIN, AND THAT WILL BY NO

156

MEANS CLEAR [THE GUILTY]; VISITING THE INIQUITY OF THE FATHERS UPON THE CHILDREN, AND UPON THE CHILDREN'S CHILDREN, UNTO THE THIRD AND TO THE FOURTH [GENERATION]. 8 AND MOSES MADE HASTE, AND BOWED HIS HEAD TOWARD THE EARTH, AND WORSHIPPED. "

GOD REVEALED HIS 13 ATTRIBUTES OF MERCY TO MOSES

[EXODUS 34:6-7 KJV] "6 AND THE LORD PASSED BY BEFORE HIM, AND PROCLAIMED, THE LORD, THE LORD GOD, MERCIFUL AND GRACIOUS, LONGSUFFERING, AND ABUNDANT IN GOODNESS AND TRUTH, 7 KEEPING MERCY FOR THOUSANDS, FORGIVING INIQUITY AND TRANSGRESSION AND SIN, AND THAT WILL BY NO MEANS CLEAR [THE GUILTY]; VISITING THE INIQUITY OF THE FATHERS UPON THE CHILDREN, AND UPON THE CHILDREN'S CHILDREN, UNTO THE THIRD AND TO THE FOURTH [GENERATION]."

The text of Exodus 34:6-7 reveals the 13 Attributes of God's Mercy. The 13 Attributes of God's Mercy are:[12]

1. The Lord! (Adonai) – God is merciful before a person sins! Even though aware that future evil lies dormant within him.

2. The Lord! (Adonai) – God is merciful after the sinner has gone astray.

3. God (El) – a Name that denotes power as ruler over nature and humankind, indicating that God's mercy sometimes surpasses even the degree indicated by this Name.

4. Compassionate – God is filled with loving sympathy for human frailty and He does not put people into situations of extreme temptation and He eases the punishment of the guilty.

5. Gracious – God shows mercy even to those who do not deserve it consoling the afflicted and raising up the oppressed.

6. Slow to anger – God gives the sinner ample time to reflect, improve, and repent.

7. Abundant in Kindness – God is kind toward those who lack personal merits, providing more gifts and blessings than they deserve; if one's personal behavior is evenly balanced between virtue and sin, God tips the scales of justice toward the good.

8. Truth – God never defaults on His word to reward those who serve Him.

9. Preserver of kindness for thousands of generations – God remembers the deeds of the righteous for the benefit of their less virtuous generations of offspring (thus we constantly invoke the merit of the Patriarchs).

10. Forgiver of iniquity – God forgives intentional sin resulting from an evil disposition, as long as the sinner repents.

11. Forgiver of willful sin – God allows even those who commit a sin with the malicious intent of rebelling against and angering Him the opportunity to

repent.

12. Forgiver of error – God forgives a sin committed out of carelessness, thoughtlessness, or apathy.

13. Who cleanses – God is merciful, gracious, and forgiving, wiping away the sins of those who truly repent; however, if one does not repent, God does not cleanse.

I will now provide you with several examples of the Bat Kol in Scripture.

PAUL RECEIVES A REVELATION OF JESUS

[ACTS 9:3-7 KJV] "3 AND AS HE JOURNEYED, HE CAME NEAR DAMASCUS: AND SUDDENLY THERE SHINED ROUND ABOUT HIM A LIGHT FROM HEAVEN: 4 AND HE FELL TO THE EARTH, AND HEARD A VOICE SAYING UNTO HIM, SAUL, SAUL, WHY PERSECUTEST THOU ME? 5 AND HE SAID, WHO ART THOU, LORD? AND THE LORD SAID, I AM JESUS WHOM THOU PERSECUTEST: [IT IS] HARD FOR THEE TO KICK AGAINST THE PRICKS. 6 AND HE TREMBLING AND ASTONISHED SAID, LORD, WHAT WILT THOU HAVE ME TO DO? AND THE LORD [SAID] UNTO HIM, ARISE, AND GO INTO THE CITY, AND IT SHALL BE TOLD THEE WHAT THOU MUST DO. 7 AND THE MEN WHICH JOURNEYED WITH HIM STOOD SPEECHLESS, HEARING A VOICE, BUT SEEING NO MAN."

Saul of Tarsus received a revelation of Jesus through the voice of the Bat Kol. The men that journeyed with him heard a voice without seeing a man.

A CERTAIN MAN OF ZORAH

[JUDGES 13:2, 9-11 KJV] "2 AND THERE WAS A CERTAIN MAN OF ZORAH, OF THE FAMILY OF THE DANITES, WHOSE NAME [WAS] MANOAH; AND HIS WIFE [WAS] BARREN, AND BARE NOT. 3 AND THE ANGEL OF THE LORD APPEARED UNTO THE WOMAN, AND SAID UNTO HER, BEHOLD NOW, THOU [ART] BARREN, AND BEAREST NOT: BUT THOU SHALT CONCEIVE, AND BEAR A SON. ... 9 AND GOD HEARKENED TO THE VOICE OF MANOAH; AND THE ANGEL OF GOD CAME AGAIN UNTO THE WOMAN AS SHE SAT IN THE FIELD: BUT MANOAH HER HUSBAND [WAS] NOT WITH HER. 10 AND THE WOMAN MADE HASTE, AND RAN, AND SHEWED HER HUSBAND, AND SAID UNTO HIM, BEHOLD, THE MAN HATH APPEARED UNTO ME, THAT CAME UNTO ME THE [OTHER] DAY. 11 AND MANOAH AROSE, AND WENT AFTER HIS WIFE, AND CAME TO THE MAN, AND SAID UNTO HIM, [ART] THOU THE MAN THAT SPAKEST UNTO THE WOMAN? AND HE SAID, I [AM]."

The Sages tell us that God spoke to Manoah and his wife through the Bat Kol. Manoah and his wife were the parents of Samson who was one of the great judges of Israel. Samson was known for his remarkable strength when the Spirit of the Lord came upon him. Manoah and his wife received the prophetic word of the birth of their son through the voice of the Bat Kol. According to the Sages, the homonymy of the word" angel" is misleading. It wasn't actually an angel that spoke to Manoah and his wife but it was the Bat Kol.

THE ANGEL IN THE FIELD

We see the Bat Kol in the life of Joseph. According to Rabbinic commentary, the voice that spoke to Joseph was the voice of the Bat Kol in Genesis 37:14-17.

[GENESIS 37:14-17 KJV] "14 AND HE SAID TO HIM, GO, I PRAY THEE, SEE WHETHER IT BE WELL WITH THY BRETHREN, AND WELL WITH THE FLOCKS; AND BRING ME WORD AGAIN. SO HE SENT HIM OUT OF THE VALE OF HEBRON, AND HE

CAME TO SHECHEM. 15 AND A CERTAIN MAN FOUND HIM, AND, BEHOLD, [HE WAS] WANDERING IN THE FIELD: AND THE MAN ASKED HIM, SAYING, WHAT SEEKEST THOU? 16 AND HE SAID, I SEEK MY BRETHREN: TELL ME, I PRAY THEE, WHERE THEY FEED [THEIR FLOCKS]. 17 AND THE MAN SAID, THEY ARE DEPARTED HENCE; FOR I HEARD THEM SAY, LET US GO TO DOTHAN. AND JOSEPH WENT AFTER HIS BRETHREN, AND FOUND THEM IN DOTHAN."

The man in the field that spoke to Joseph in Shechem was the voice of the Bat Kol.

.

Rivalry between two Houses of Judaism

The Talmud (Eruvin 13b) tells us about the rival schools of Judaism. The House of Hillel and the House of Shammai debated whose authority was to be accepted in Jewish law.[14]

The debate was resolved by the Bat Kol which decided that the actual ruling would be in line with the House of Hillel. Rabban Hillel and Rabban Shammai were two leading sages in the last century BC to the first part of the 1st century.

The House of Hillel was generally more lenient than the House of Shammai in their rulings. For example, the House of Hillel would permit anyone to study Torah including Gentiles. The House of Shammai would not permit "non-worthy" students to study Torah.

In summary, the Bat Kol typically provides God's will or judgment. We heard God's will in the examples of Jesus' baptism and at the Mount of Transfiguration. We saw God's judgment upon Saul of Tarsus (Paul) for his persecution of Christians. We saw God's judgment in favor of the House of Hillel. These are all examples of the Bat Kol. Let's pray that the Lord will reveal His Voice to you.

PRAYER TO HEAR THE VOICE OF GOD

"HEAVENLY FATHER, I ASK YOU TO REVEAL YOUR MAGNIFICENT VOICE TO THE READERS OF THIS BOOK. I ASK YOU TO REVEAL YOUR WILL AND SPEAK TO THE READERS IN EVERY AREA OF THEIR LIVES FROM THE MOST MINISCULE TO THE MOST SIGNIFICANT AREAS OF THEIR LIVES. SPEAK TO MY FRIENDS IN THE EARTH, IN THE WIND, IN THE FIRE, AND IN THE STILL SMALL VOICE. WE ASK THIS IN JESUS' NAME."

Jesus said that everyone who asks will receive and whoever seeks will find.

[MATTHEW 7:7-8 NKJV] 7 "ASK, AND IT WILL BE GIVEN TO YOU; SEEK, AND YOU WILL FIND; KNOCK, AND IT WILL BE OPENED TO YOU. 8 "FOR EVERYONE WHO ASKS RECEIVES, AND HE WHO SEEKS FINDS, AND TO HIM WHO KNOCKS IT WILL BE OPENED.

God is giving you one of the greatest gifts and that is the gift of hearing His Voice. Thank you so much for joining me on this journey.

ABOUT THE AUTHOR

SANJAY PRAJAPATI is a pastor, author, teacher, and a public speaker. He began studying Torah under the mantle of Dr. Michelle Corral, foundress of Breath of the Ministry Ministries in 1991. He currently serves as the Assistant Pastor at Breath of the Spirit Ministries.

Sanjay's philosophy is that the Torah is the foundation of all Scripture, including the Hebrew and New Testament Scriptures. He teaches a weekly Torah service entitled Destined4Torah in addition to other weekly services.

He also was a guest speaker on several telecasts including Dr. Corral's weekly program, The Prophetic Word, which currently airs on the Word Network.

He is the author of two books, <u>The Final Countdown</u> and <u>Earth, Wind, Fire, & A Still Small Voice</u>.

His mission is to reveal the depths of the Bible through Torah study and to show that the Bible is not a memoir of past events. The Bible speaks to people of all generations and in all walks of life. His personal motto is: "The blueprint to your destiny is found in lives of Biblical Figures."

Sanjay and his wife, Bhavna live in Orange County, CA.

Amplify Your Life - Subscribe to Sanjay Prajapati

YouTube: http://www.youtube.com/user/Destined4Torah
Facebook: http://www.facebook.com/Destined4Torah
Twitter: https://twitter.com/Destined4Torah
Instagram: https://www.instagram.com/Destined4Torah
Blog: http://www.destined4torah.com

Amazon Author Page:

http://www.Amazon.com/author/sanjayprajapati

Book Sanjay To Speak At Your Event!

Book Sanjay Prajapati as your Keynote Speaker and You are Guaranteed to Make Your Event Unforgettable!

For over ten years, Sanjay Prajapati has been teaching Torah to people from all walks of life to help them build their relationship with God and to discover God's designed purpose for their lives. His students have included pastors, priests, and laypeople. He uses weekly Torah services, online video, social media, and television guest appearances to spread his message. He makes Torah concepts easy to comprehend and apply.

Sanjay's love for the Torah began in 1991 while attending Dr. Michelle Corral's ministry. He discovered his purpose in Dr. Corral's Torah services and he has consequently become passionate about spreading the knowledge and prophetic depths of Torah to the world.

His unique style inspires, empowers, and entertains audiences while giving them the tools and strategies they need to discover and implement the blueprint to their destinies.

For more info, visit www.Destined4Torah.com or call +1 (714) 922-0414.

ONE LAST THING...

If you enjoyed this book or found it useful, then I would be very grateful if you will post a short review on Amazon. Your support really does make a difference and I read all the reviews personally, so I can get your feedback and make this book even better.

To leave a review, go to the following Amazon link:

- http://www.Amazon.com/author/sanjayprajapati
- Click on this book's title
- Click on "Write a Customer Review"

Thanks again for your support!

CITED RESOURCES

[i] Jungreis, Y., Jungreis, O., & Jungreis, E. (2009). *Torah for your table.* Brooklyn, NY: Shaar Press.

[ii] Bereishit - Genesis - Chapter 1 (Parshah Bereishit). (n.d.). Retrieved January 02, 2018, from http://www.chabad.org/library/bible_cdo/aid/8165/jewish/Chapter-1.htm

[iii] Scherman, N., & Zlotowitz, M. (1978). Yonah: a new translation with a commentary anthologized from Talmudic, Midrashic and Rabbinic sources. Brooklyn (N.Y.): Mesorah Publications.

[iv] Munk, E., & Kirzner, Y. (1992). The Call of the Torah: 5 - Devarim an anthology of interpretation and commentary on the five books of Moses. Brooklyn, NY: Mesorah Publications.

[v] Grubb, Norman. (1952). Rees Howell Intercessor (Kindle). CLC Publications. Kindle Edition. Lutterworth Press.

[5] Eisemann, Rabbi Moshe. (1989). Yechezkel / Ezekiel a new translation with a commentary

anthologized from Talmudic, Midrashic, and Rabbinic sources. Brooklyn, NY: ArtScroll Mesorah Publications..

[6] Merkabah. (2017, December 14). Retrieved January 03, 2018, from http://en.wikipedia.org/wiki/Merkabah

[7] Jewish angelic hierarchy. (2017, December 27). Retrieved January 03, 2018, from https://en.wikipedia.org/wiki/Jewish_angelic_hierarchy

[8] Further Elaboration of Ezekiel's Vision. (n.d.). Retrieved January 04, 2018, from https://www.ou.org/torah/machshava/the-god-papers/31-elaboration-ezekiels-vision/

[15] Munk, M. L. (2012). *The wisdom in the Hebrew alphabet: the sacred letters as a guide to Jewish deed and thought.* Brooklyn, NY: Mesorah Publications.

[9] Throw under the bus. (2017, October 30). Retrieved January 05, 2018, from https://en.wikipedia.org/wiki/Throw_under_the_bus

[10] Gersonides. (2017, December 21). Retrieved January 05, 2018, from https://en.wikipedia.org/wiki/Gersonides

[11] Twelve Minor Prophets. (2018, January 04). Retrieved January 05, 2018, from https://en.wikipedia.org/wiki/Twelve_Minor_Prophets

[12] Eisenberg, R. L. (n.d.). The 13 Attributes of Mercy. Retrieved January 02, 2018, from https://www.myjewishlearning.com/article/the-13-attributes-of-mercy/2/

[14] Jacobs, R. L. (n.d.). Bat Kol - A Divine Voice. Retrieved January 05, 2018, from http://www.myjewishlearning.com/article/bat-kol-a-divine-voice/

Made in the USA
Lexington, KY
08 August 2018